Praise for **Learning to Live in the Dark**

"In *Learning to Live in the Dark,* Wen Stephenson confronts our on-going planetary crisis in all its horrifying bleakness. But even as he looks into the abyss Stephenson is able to find rays of light within the darkness. This is a book for anyone searching for meaning and hope in an age of crisis." —**Amitav Ghosh**, author of *The Nutmeg's Curse: Parables for a Planet in Crisis*

"Wen Stephenson has long been not only one of the ablest thinkers about the climate crisis, but one of the most determined do-ers—an unyielding activist in the fights he describes so well. That makes this an important account on many scores, one that will nourish and sustain you!" —**Bill McKibben**, founder of 350.org and Third Act; author of *Here Comes the Sun*

"It's ironic and paradoxical that Stephenson would name his latest offering *Learning to Live in the Dark* when there is so much light in this book that elucidates contradictions through an illumination of bold and requisite veracity. These essays deliver on what it will take to retain collective humanity in an epoch of climate catastrophe that demands the politics of solidarity and complexity rather than comfort and deference." —**Anthony Karefa Rogers-Wright**, climate and racial justice advocate; author of *Good Friday: The Death of the US Climate Movement and Pathways For Its Resurrection* (forthcoming)

"To search beneath the surface, reflect deeply on what one has found, and write with a fierce honesty about it; that is the path of the finest journalists. You will find that in Wen Stephenson's essays. His journey is an inspiration." —**James Gustave "Gus" Speth**, Distinguished Fellow, The Democracy Collaborative; author of *They Knew: The US Federal Government's Fifty-Year Role in Causing the Climate Crisis*

"Stephenson's approach to the human crisis speaks volumes to me. He knows it is a matter of heart as well as mind. His writer-heroes overlap with my own because they are morally clear and unafraid. Stephenson too is unafraid." —**Todd Gitlin** (1943-2022), Columbia University, author of *The Sixties: Years of Hope, Days of Rage*

Learning to Live in the Dark

ESSAYS IN A TIME OF CATASTROPHE

WEN STEPHENSON

Haymarket Books
Chicago, IL

© 2025 Wen Stephenson
Published in 2025 by
Haymarket Books
P.O. Box 180165
Chicago, IL 60618
www.haymarketbooks.org

ISBN: 979-888890-375-9

Distributed to the trade in the US through Consortium Book Sales
and Distribution (www.cbsd.com) and internationally through In-
gram Publisher Services International (www.ingramcontent.com).

This book was published with the generous support of Lannan Foundation, Wallace Action Fund, and Marguerite Casey Foundation.

Special discounts are available for bulk purchases by organizations
and institutions. Please email info@haymarketbooks.org for more
information.

Cover photograph by John D. Jackson.
Cover design by Matt Avery.

Printed in Canada by union labor.

Library of Congress Cataloging-in-Publication data is available.

10 9 8 7 6 5 4 3 2 1

For Fiona,
always

And in memory of my parents,
Patsy Jo (Ferguson) Stephenson and
Oliver Wendell Stephenson

For if I do not love them as they are, it will not be they whom I love, and my love will be unreal.
—Simone Weil, letter to Fr. Joseph-Marie Perrin

§

We're working for something that brings us together beyond blasphemies and prayers. It's all that matters.
—Albert Camus, *The Plague*

CONTENTS

PART THREE: On the Other Side of Despair

AUTHOR'S NOTE

All of the previously published essays here have been revised, and some have been expanded, but I have deliberately left references to details and events of the moment in which they were written unaltered, without updates. I've done this so as not to distort either the record of, or my response to, the situation in which each essay took shape. The reader may judge how much, if at all, the situation has since changed.

"Truly, I live in dark times!"

"Truly, I live in dark times!" So begins Bertolt Brecht's anguished and indelible poem "To Those Born After" (or "To Posterity"), written in Denmark in the late 1930s while he was on the run, as a prominent German leftist, from Hitler's Third Reich. "You who will emerge again from the flood / In which we have gone under," Brecht addresses his imagined reader, "Remember / When you speak of our failings / The dark time too / Which you have escaped."

At the time he wrote the poem, Brecht still advocated a utopian Marxist-Leninist future beyond class and national conflict, but not without misgivings. He was aware by then of Stalin's terror and the Moscow show trials, and that his own artistic commitments put him at risk, and the poem is that rare thing in Brecht—a confessional, conscience-stricken, conflicted tale of failed revolutionary ends and means, of humanity betrayed in the effort to save it. And so in a final appeal, holding to some desperate faith, he writes, "When the time comes at last / And man is a helper to man / Think on us / With forbearance."

I am far removed from the time and place, and the historical struggle, in which that poem was written, but it haunts me in ways I find hard to articulate.

Brecht was among the men and women profiled by Hannah Arendt in her 1968 volume of essays, *Men in Dark Times*, and despite the bleakness, even despair, of Brecht's famous poem, Arendt found something in it worth holding on to, something affirming, something worth examining—a warning, a self-knowledge—in her effort to understand the source and meaning of the poet's witness. "That even in the darkest of times we have the right to expect some illumination," Arendt explained in her introduction, "and that such illumination may well come less from theories and concepts than from the uncertain, flickering, and often weak light that some men and women, in their lives and their works, will kindle under almost all circumstances and shed over the time span that was given them on earth—this conviction is the inarticulate background against which these profiles were drawn."

I make no attempt to imitate Hannah Arendt in what follows, but I do offer the essays here in much the same spirit conjured in those introductory lines. We, too, live in dark times—even, perhaps, among the darkest. And we need, crave, seek, some kind of illumination.

§

Written over a period of eight years, beginning in 2016, and intended to be read as a series, these essays concern themselves with a not-so-distant past, an embattled present, and a future that, while impossible to know in its particulars, is nevertheless increasingly circumscribed by catastrophic ecological breakdown and social instability. The geophysical forces unleashed by the carbon-fueled warming of Earth's atmosphere—combined with the political forces of denialist capital and various racial and ethno-religious nationalisms—already create a situation in which forms of political and social evil, on a scale not seen since the middle of the twentieth century, have come into view.

The necessity of naming these evils is among the convictions animating this book. How to live into this time, while holding on to those aspects of our humanity that can salvage and sustain any sort of just community, is the book's central question. In what follows, I look back to Arendt and other twentieth-century Europeans (Václav Havel, Simone Weil, Albert Camus), and one who rebelled against European colonialism (Frantz Fanon), and back to the nineteenth century in America (Thoreau) and Russia (Dostoevsky), while also considering some of our contemporaries writing about and engaging in the struggles of our own moment. If these writers and thinkers share any one thing in common—aside from fierce intelligence and a willingness, even a need, to face the most harrowing facts of their times—it's the aspiration toward something like a universal humanism, whether secular or religious, and ultimately transcending both. All are in search of what I'd call, without embarrassment, human solidarity and its sources.

But if it's comfort or some kind of cost-free hope you're looking for, be warned that these essays make no such promises. What they do, when read together as a whole, is peer straight into the abyss of our converging political and planetary catastrophes, coming at it from varying angles, historical and literary, collective and individual, political and moral and spiritual, at times deeply personal, seeking insight from others who learned—or tried—to live in the dark. (It may be that the best we can ever do is try—and keep trying.) They trace a personal and political arc from my first attempt to fully face the abyss, with the help of Arendt, in the first year of the Trump era; through a renewed political engagement with the climate-justice movement and my ongoing commitment to escalated nonviolent direct action; through a personal and spiritual reckoning in the depths of the pandemic and the violent aftermath of the 2020 US election; and on up to the reckoning of a genocidal war in Palestine and the dark, chaotic uncertainty of 2024.

This book was written before the outcome of the US election could be known, but make no mistake: even the best imaginable result would not have "saved" us—there is no American center-left solution to our global climate and political emergency—and a second Trump presidency only points to what we already knew, that the United States faces the very real threat of white-nationalist "Christian" fascism. The latter has been clear, to those with ears to hear and eyes to see, for the past eight years, if not the past century, and it is among the underlying currents running through these essays. And so this book, given these combined realities, keeps returning to a question that now seems to resonate with all the more urgency, especially on the left: If nothing short of revolution, in some form, can salvage the possibility of a better world—ecologically and socially—and yet if a viable revolutionary mass movement is nowhere to be found, then what does a life of radical commitment look like in the face of catastrophes that will not, do not, wait?

Will those born after, if they emerge from the flood, ask why we did not fight more forcefully?

§

Several of these essays are quite personal, and I should perhaps say something about where I'm coming from, my own experience, my own stake. This book is written not merely by a journalist or essayist or activist, or by a white, straight, cisgender man, born and raised in Southern California with a working-class, rural Texas, evangelical Christian family background. I am all of these, and I fully acknowledge the privileged yet complex position from which I write—not least in that, like most readers of this book, I am also an educated, housed, well-fed Global Northerner and beneficiary of empire.

But such terms and labels say nothing about the inner life of the one writing, about the psychological, emotional, spiritual, even physical toll of wrestling for many years with the questions raised here and with the responsibilities and choices required of one who takes them seriously. Maybe I'm not supposed to admit this, especially as a person of privilege (What are my struggles compared to those of the earth's oppressed?), but in early 2016, after the publication of my book on the US climate movement—and as the world watched the rise of Donald Trump and the surge of white "Christian" nationalism—I fell into a vertiginous depression, not for the first or last time, intensified by my long struggle with anxiety and addiction (I've been sober for nearly two decades, but addiction, like anxiety, is never cured). I didn't know if I would write or engage in activism ever again, and I confess—this is not easy—that I questioned my reasons and my desire to live. It was in those darkest moments that I picked up Arendt and Camus, Weil and Dostoevsky, Havel and Fanon, and many others not in this book—Bonhoeffer, Wiesel, Levi, Miłosz, Solzhenitsyn, and more—who faced the abyss in their time. And I began to read them, or reread them, in earnest. That's how this book was born, as though I was trying to read and write my way out of real despair. I won't bullshit you—I don't know if I've succeeded. But I've chosen to live, and to fight, and to go down fighting.

If these essays, as my own sort of confession, my appeal to posterity, reveal a constant internal struggle between despair in the face of our predicament and something like, not any cheap hope, but what might be called *resolve*—and if the struggle has no satisfying end, so that despair and resolve live side by side, unreconciled—then the book I've written is an honest one.

Where precisely the resolve comes from, how to find it, how to hold on to it—and why—may be unknowable. All that matters is that the resolve is real—every bit as real as the dark itself.

PART ONE

Catastrophes Converge

ONE

Learning to Live in the Dark

Reading Arendt in the Anthropocene

SEPTEMBER 2017

. . . even in the darkest of times we have the right to expect some illumination . . .
—Hannah Arendt, *Men in Dark Times* (1968)

1.

The minister that Sunday morning asked me what I most fear losing. For her, she said, as if embarrassed, confessing, it's the seasons—the way we knew them when we were young, in our bones, the way our parents and their parents knew them. It was a rainy autumn day in New York City, October of 2016, and water dripped from yellowing leaves.

For me, the answer came without hesitation, because I think about it all the time. Humanity, I told her. Friendship, solidarity, love of neighbor. That's what I'm afraid of losing. Because what I fear most is what we're capable of doing to each other, and of not doing for each other, when, as Hannah Arendt would say, the chips are down—when it's dark outside, and we let the darkness in. Because, let there be no doubt, it's getting very dark.

How dark? Put it this way: Some four-fifths of what used to be called the "permanent" sea ice covering the Arctic Ocean is now gone. The stability of the global climate system, as we know it, depends largely on the Arctic, warming at a rate no model projected, spiraling toward worst-case scenarios decades sooner than predicted. What was once unthinkable destruction is now all but guaranteed, first and foremost among the world's poorest people, the majority of the human population.

In the face of this situation, even as waves of refugees fleeing drought and war destabilize Europe, a right-wing populist movement propels a quasi-fascist, science-denying demagogue to the presidency of the most powerful nation on Earth. Among his first acts is to name as secretary of state the man who had only recently been chief executive of the largest oil and gas corporation on the planet—a corporation that has long understood the findings of climate scientists yet has deceived the public and obstructed any serious response for decades, while pursuing plans to drill in the melted Arctic.

These are baseline facts, the actual conditions of the world in which we live. Two catastrophes, planetary and political, converge; humanity approaches geophysical and social tipping points unimagined by previous generations. With the victory of the carbon-industrial machine, it is now clear, we confront corporate and political forces not only racist in ideology but totalitarian in mindset and ambition, if not yet in methods. Unless, as to methods, it can be argued that to ensure the suffering and death of countless innocent millions, entire countries and cultures, by means of lies and the obstruction of urgent life-saving measures, marks some kind of epochal advance in the art of administrative mass murder—what amounts, in many places, to something like genocide.

There are no historical analogies to be drawn here, no direct comparisons. We live in the present. And yet, "no comparisons" does not mean "no insights," no lessons to be sought. There are no borders in human history that are closed, no human experience walled off from an authentic human effort to understand. And I confess that when I try to make sense of this picture, to fit the facts we are facing, planetary and political—the true scale of the unprecedented crimes now unfolding—into any accepted category, I'm at a loss, the mind reels, and I reach for the past.

2.

The opening lines of Hannah Arendt's short, bracing preface to the first edition of *The Origins of Totalitarianism*, published in 1951, capture the mood of a generation that had lived through two cataclysmic world wars, experienced economic collapse, revolutions, and "homelessness on an unprecedented scale," and now faced the prospect of an all-destroying third world war. The mood is one of exhaustion, uncertainty, a dull and ever-present fear. "This moment of anticipation," she writes, "is like the calm that settles after all hopes have died. . . . Never has our future been more unpredictable, never have we depended so much on political forces that cannot be trusted to follow the rules of common sense and self-interest—forces that look like sheer insanity, if judged by the standards of other centuries."

Arendt's words in those first pages—with their slight awkwardness, the not-entirely-confident English of a German Jewish émigré who held proudly to the mother tongue—carry a weight I can only guess at. Warning against the tendency of her contemporaries to look numbly away, to minimize the horrors, to move on, she insists upon squarely confronting the new facts, if only to try to comprehend them. The kind of comprehension she has in mind, though, would come not by taking refuge in old "commonplaces."

It requires, she writes, "examining and bearing consciously the burden which our century has placed on us—neither denying its existence nor submitting meekly to its weight."

For Arendt, as a midcentury European Jew, that burden was all but overwhelming. Looking back on the moment when she and her husband, Heinrich Blücher, got the first reports in New York about Auschwitz, she later told interviewer Günter Gaus: "That was in 1943. And at first we didn't believe it. . . . It was really as if an abyss had opened. . . . *This ought not to have happened.* And I don't mean just the number of victims. I mean the method, the fabrication of corpses and so on. . . . Something happened there to which we cannot reconcile ourselves. None of us ever can." But the reality, the forces that opened the abyss, could still be—had to be—described, analyzed, judged.

Central to Arendt's analysis is her acute observation that totalitarian movements, and later fully realized regimes, require the construction of a "fictitious world," as seen in their "conspicuous disdain for the whole texture of reality." Writing in 1954, between the first and the significantly revised 1958 edition of *Origins*, she observed: "Insofar as [totalitarian] ideological thinking is independent of existing reality, it looks upon all factuality as fabricated, and therefore no longer knows any reliable criterion for distinguishing truth from falsehood."

This is crucial, and not only as a premonition of the way today's far right seems to adopt (and distort) postmodern theory to construct a world of "alternative facts." For Arendt, it's the key that unlocks the totalitarian mindset. Noting that "it would be quite possible for totalitarian rulers or the men immediately surrounding them not to believe in the actual content of their preaching," she sees through the delusions of a new generation of leaders, which has somehow, it seems to her, "lost even the ability to distinguish between such believing and nonbelieving." At which point, she draws the all-important line from belief in nothing to belief in *anything*:

> Underlying these beliefs or nonbelief . . . is another belief shared by all totalitarian rulers, as well as by people thinking and acting along totalitarian lines. This is the belief in the omnipotence of *man* and at the same time of the superfluity of *men*; it is the belief that everything is permitted and, much more terrible, that everything is possible.

In the last chapter of *Origins*, Arendt dwells on this relationship between delusions of unlimited possibility and the need to fabricate a reality to fit the ideological pattern. The totalitarian leaders' "faith in human omnipotence . . . carries them into experiments which human imaginations may have outlined but human activity certainly never realized." Meanwhile, "normal men," those outside the totalitarian world and its mindset, "refuse to believe their eyes and ears in the face of the monstrous" and engage in the kind of "wishful thinking" that only "shirks reality in the face of real insanity."

Arendt found the essence of the truly monstrous in that concept of superfluity. Totalitarianism, as distinguished from "mere" tyranny or dictatorship, "strives not toward despotic rule over men, but toward a system in which men are superfluous." That is, a system in which human beings, both as individuals and distinct groups, become surplus, unnecessary and unwanted, cease to have any intrinsic value as human beings—are dehumanized. When that happens, the standards by which human beings explain and judge relations among themselves fall apart, and we're faced with something truly radical, incomprehensible:

> Until now the totalitarian belief that everything is pos-
> sible seems to have proved only that everything can be
> destroyed. . . . When the impossible was made possible
> it became the unpunishable, unforgivable absolute evil
> which could no longer be understood and explained by
> the evil motives of self-interest, greed, covetousness, re-
> sentment, lust for power, and cowardice. . . . Therefore, we
> actually have nothing to fall back on in order to under-
> stand a phenomenon that nevertheless confronts us with
> its overpowering reality and breaks down all standards we
> know.

With nothing to fall back on, no recognizable standards by
which to comprehend and judge, anything can happen, anything
might be justified, in the future. All bets are off.

What comprehensible motive could there be for poisoning
the well from which one's own children must drink, much less the
atmosphere itself? What kind of mindset makes one's own children and grandchildren—and everyone else's, indeed all future
generations—superfluous?

The terrifying threat of the totalitarian systems for present and
future generations, Arendt warns at the conclusion of *Origins*, "is
that today, with populations and homelessness everywhere on the
increase, masses of people are continuously rendered superfluous
if we continue to think of our world in utilitarian terms." In other
words, she writes with trademark bluntness in this starkest of conclusions, "Totalitarian solutions may well survive the fall of totalitarian regimes."

You might argue that Arendt overstated her warning, that her fear proved unfounded, that history has seen no recurrence of "totalitarian solutions," at least on such a vast scale, that the world has in fact become more democratic, more prosperous, less violent; that technology and markets will solve hunger and war, that extreme poverty will be eliminated within our lifetimes; that we have moved decisively away from Arendt's dark vision. Indeed, many believers in the march of progress do still say such things, while ignoring, dismissing, or outright denying the scientific reality of the melted Arctic and the ever-rising concentration of atmospheric carbon, as well as the political reality of the carbon-industrial machine. In fact, in Arendt's image of populations continuously rendered superfluous, she arrived at an insight the lasting importance of which only time could reveal. In her effort to face and comprehend, as few others could or would, the darkness of her historical moment—the forces that opened the abyss—Arendt anticipated our own.

Writing at the moment when lofty debates concerning "human rights" were in the air, and attempts were made at universal definitions and declarations, Arendt points to the hollowness of the concept at the international level, when states were confronted with uprooted, homeless masses. It turns out, Arendt observes, that the "Rights of Man" require a polity to guarantee them. "We became aware of the existence of a right to have rights . . . and a right to belong to some kind of organized community only when millions of people emerged who had lost and could not regain these rights because of the new global political situation." There appeared suddenly unprecedented waves of stateless people who had lost the status of citizenship and were left stranded by an international order that had no place for them. "The conception of human rights . . . broke down," Arendt observes, "at the very moment when those who professed to believe in it were for the first time confronted with people who had indeed lost all other qualities and specific relationships—except that they were still human. The world found nothing sacred in the abstract nakedness of being human."

§

Arendt knew something of what she wrote—understood enough about that nakedness to know there's nothing abstract about it, that her oxymoronic phrase only pointed up the absurdity of the situation in which she, too, had been caught. She herself had been a refugee, homeless and stateless.

But Arendt's story, while harrowing, turned out to be one of absurdly good luck. She narrowly escaped from Nazi Germany, along with her mother, in the spring of 1933, at the age of twenty-six, after the Reichstag fire and Hitler's consolidation of power made clear that staying was untenable. Apolitical in her youth, she had been awakened into action by the Nazi victory that January, sheltering fugitive Communists and other members of the German Left in her apartment as they escaped the country in a kind of "underground railroad" operation, and she took on covert work conducting research on antisemitism at the National Library. She was soon arrested, held for eight days, and questioned by a German policeman who turned out to be sympathetic and found a way to let her go. (She later described the German police officer as a "charming fellow" who "had some misgivings" and that his "open, honest face" convinced her to trust him with her life.)

Once released, Arendt knew such luck couldn't hold, and she and her mother hastily gathered the few things they could carry with them and fled Germany by way of a secret border station in the south, heading to Prague, then Geneva, and finally to Paris. There, she fell in with a group of fellow German émigrés, including her soon-to-be second husband and lifelong soulmate, the independent leftist scholar Heinrich Blücher.

When the war came, and the Germans advanced on Paris, Arendt and Blücher were separated and, like other German refugees, interned as "enemy aliens" by the French. In mid-May 1940, Arendt was transported to an internment camp for women at Gurs far to the south, in view of the Pyrenees—and in the weeks that followed, she confronted despair. According to her biographer, Elisabeth Young-Bruehl, Arendt confided to a friend years later that during this time she had seriously contemplated taking her own life—and, having earnestly considered the question, decided resolutely against. It was a good choice. In the chaotic days following the French defeat in mid-June, Arendt and about two hundred other women (out of some seven thousand interned) seized a fleeting opportunity to leave the camp, though without legal protection and, for most, with nowhere to go. Nearly all the women who stayed behind, preferring what seemed the relative security of Gurs, were ultimately sent by the Germans to death camps in the east.

Arendt and Blücher were reunited, as though miraculously, on the streets of Montauban in southern France. The two of them, by then married and able to secure American "emergency visas" in Marseilles, made their escape from the country in the spring of 1941, with transit visas through Spain to Portugal and the port at Lisbon, where they sailed for New York.

One of Arendt's and Blücher's best friends from Paris would not be so fortunate. "Walter Benjamin took his own life on September 29 in Portbou on the Spanish frontier," Arendt wrote from Montauban on October 21, 1940, to Benjamin's close friend Gershom Scholem, whom she had met in Paris years earlier. "Jews are dying in Europe," reads the last line of her terse, almost telegraphic letter, "and are being buried like dogs."

Unable to get a French exit visa, Benjamin had decided to take his chances on the overland route through the Pyrenees and across the border at Portbou, which the French were known to leave unguarded. Arendt and Blücher were with Benjamin in Marseilles just before he set out with a small group for the journey on foot across the frontier, and he was apparently not in good health, physically or emotionally. Benjamin, Arendt believed, probably arrived at Portbou "in a state of serious exhaustion," only to find that the Spanish border was closed and that his party would have to return to France the next day. That night Benjamin took a lethal dose of morphine, "whereupon the border officials, upon whom this suicide had made an impression," Arendt writes in her essay about him in *Men in Dark Times*, "allowed his companions to proceed to Portugal." Soon thereafter, the French began issuing visas again.

Benjamin entrusted several unpublished manuscripts to Arendt before leaving Marseilles, among them his *Theses on the Philosophy of History*, one of his last major pieces. Arendt was struck by Benjamin's gnomic theses, especially number IX, in which he conjures an image of the "angel of history," inspired by a Paul Klee painting, with its face "turned toward the past." Benjamin writes, "Where we perceive a chain of events, he sees one single catastrophe which keeps piling wreckage upon wreckage." In Benjamin's apocalyptic vision, the angel wants to "awaken the dead, and make whole what has been smashed," but a storm is blowing from the direction of the past, out of Paradise, and it "irresistibly propels him into the future to which his back is turned, while the pile of debris before him grows skyward." Benjamin identifies the storm as "what we call progress." Arendt, who quotes the passage at length in her own essay, remarks simply that "nothing could be more 'undialectic'"—indeed, the notion that Benjamin's way of thinking "should ever have bothered with a consistent, dialectically sensible, rationally explainable process seems absurd." Benjamin, she notes, thought like a poet—or, she might have added, a prophet.

In her essay, Arendt goes on to quote a 1935 letter of Benjamin's from Paris. "Naturally," he wrote, "one must wish for the planet that one day it will experience a civilization that has abandoned blood and horror." Yet he found it "terribly doubtful" that his generation, or any, would bring such a thing about. "And if we don't," he went on, "the planet will finally punish us, its unthoughtful well-wishers, by presenting us with the Last Judgment."

Writing to Scholem from New York in October 1941, Arendt recalled, "Months later, when we arrived at Portbou, we searched in vain for his grave. It was nowhere to be found. His name was nowhere." They looked in the cemetery, carved into terraces on a hillside overlooking "a small bay, directly onto the Mediterranean. . . . By far one of the most fantastically beautiful places I've ever seen." Today, a memorial stands there for Benjamin at the edge of the sea.

§

When the international order has failed, when fine sentiments concerning human rights have proven meaningless in the face of naked humanity, human beings stripped of community, of political and legal status, possessing only, as Arendt writes in *Origins*, "those qualities which . . . must remain unqualified, mere existence"—that is, when the abyss has opened up—Arendt asks if truly nothing at all remains on which mere human beings may rely.

Her answer surprises me, stops me, catches me off guard. When all else is lost, Arendt writes:

> This mere existence, that is, all that which is mysteriously given us by birth and which includes the shape of our bodies and the talents of our minds, can be adequately dealt

with only by the unpredictable hazards of friendship and sympathy, or by the great and incalculable grace of love, which says with Augustine, '*Volo ut sis* (I want you to be),' without being able to give any particular reason for such supreme and unsurpassable affirmation.

Of course Arendt knew that such affirmation, this grace beyond reason, can be surpassingly rare, unreliable, and unexpected, like a sudden flare, an unforeseen beacon, in the dark. And yet no less real for all of that.

3.

The world finds nothing sacred in the mere existence of a Syrian refugee washed up on a beach; in the undocumented persons, "illegals," jailed and deported. It found nothing sacred in the prayerful faces and freezing bodies at Standing Rock; in the Far Rockaways or the Lower Ninth Ward when the storm surge came; in Houston's toxic flood waters; or in south Florida or the Leeward Islands, stripped bare by a lethal wind.

On April 28, 2016, with such images in mind, I sat staring at the cold, white, concrete wall of a Boston jail cell. By coincidence, it was my daughter's twelfth birthday, and I had just placed my body in the way of an eighteen-wheeled flatbed at the entrance to a construction site of a high-pressure, fracked-gas pipeline through a residential neighborhood of West Roxbury, as part of a sustained grassroots campaign in which hundreds engaged in similar actions. When the police officer on detail ordered me and my companions to move, we politely refused and were arrested, cuffed, and placed in the back of a BPD wagon. The charge was disturbing the peace. Whose peace, precisely, we had disturbed at the entrance to a construction site was never clear. Maybe the truck driver's. Maybe the cop's.

Now I sat by myself on the steel bed of a six-by-ten cell and stared at the wall. As I had never been in such a situation (despite my best previous efforts), the only thing that occurred to me was what a sheltered and privileged life I had led, and I wondered about the other individuals who'd sat in that space, and what, if anything, they'd done to deserve being there, and what they would think of me, this pretender, interloper, poseur.

I spent only a few hours without my freedom, and the charges were dropped, but I can't get the cell door's dull metallic clank, as it shut, out of my head: its inescapable pronouncement of my bodily insignificance, my frail and finite physicality. I've known and worked alongside people in recent years who've done real jail time, gone to prison, in some cases risked their lives, to halt even briefly the carbon-industrial machine, to be the sand in the gears— to impede pipelines, coal shipments, the desecration of Indigenous land, the poisoning of brown and Black and white bodies living in proximity of the power plants, refineries, and mines—and I knew the absurd puniness of my gesture toward solidarity with the powerless and suffering. And as always, there was the question why— the question of whether such gestures still make any sense in the face of all we now know; of whether it's time to accept the futility of actions that depend, for their effect, on the compassion, or conscience, or humanity, of those whom they address. Whether more force, more sacrifice, is now required. The question: What kind of resistance is possible against a world without mercy?

And even as I form those words, the familiar voice in my head: *Who am I to judge? Who do I think I am? Am I not complicit—aren't we all—even sitting in jail?*

I want to be honest. Maybe this ever-present sense of complicity, of guilt, is the reason I felt in the end so oddly at peace, my conscience salved, as I sat there facing the white and changeless wall. Not because I'd performed some difficult, noble act—I had not—but because I was certain that jail was where I belonged. Because there, at last, in that dank, windowless cell, I was removed from my life in the world, from society, contact with others—so that, finally, to my indescribable relief, I was a danger to no one. It was as though, for those few hours, I could do no harm—to the planet or to people. As if, albeit briefly, I had somehow in my isolation disappeared.

§

"There exists in our society a widespread fear of judging that has nothing whatever to do with the biblical 'Judge not, that ye not be judged,'" Arendt writes in the manuscript of a 1964 address titled "Personal Responsibility Under Dictatorship." Rather, she notes there, "behind the unwillingness to judge lurks the suspicion that no one is a free agent, and hence the doubt that anyone is responsible or could be expected to answer for what he has done." As soon as anyone raises moral issues, she observes sharply, the one who raises them is met "with a kind of mock-modesty that in saying, Who am I to judge? actually means We're all alike, equally bad, and those who try, or pretend that they try, to remain halfway decent are either saints or hypocrites, and in either case should leave us alone."

This aversion to making judgments which Arendt identified in her generation—and which is equally if not more familiar to intellectuals and writers of my own (so-called post-Boomers, the unfortunately named Gen X)—is closely connected to the distinction she draws between responsibility and guilt, and what she called the "well-known fallacy" of "collective guilt." In a 1968 lecture called "Collective Responsibility," she puts it like this: "There is such a thing as responsibility for things one has not done; one can be held liable for them. But there is no such thing as being or feeling guilty for things that happened without oneself actively participating in them." In the case of postwar Germany, Arendt writes, "the cry 'We are all guilty' that at first hearing sounded so very noble and tempting has actually only served to exculpate to a considerable degree those who actually were guilty. Where all are guilty, nobody is."

As Arendt notes elsewhere, this sentiment of collective guilt echoed, with an unintentional and bitter irony, Adolf Eichmann's own defense. In the closing pages of *Eichmann in Jerusalem*, where she addresses him posthumously, she writes, "[You said] that almost anybody could have taken your place, so that potentially almost all Germans are equally guilty. What you meant to say was that where all, or almost all, are guilty, nobody is." Or as she puts it in that 1968 lecture, in the case of postwar Germans who indulged in what she called the "phony sentimentality" of collective guilt, "the cry 'We are all guilty' is actually a declaration of solidarity with the wrongdoers."

Of course Eichmann's defense, along with that of other senior Nazi murderers, was always by design, always part of the plan. One of Arendt's darkest observations in *Origins* concerns the ways in which totalitarianism attempts to make all members of the society complicit, so that "the consciously organized complicity of all men in the crimes of totalitarian regimes is extended to the victims and thus made really total." Conditions are created in which "[t]he alternative is no longer between good and evil, but between murder and murder." But this does not mean that all are equally guilty. The conditions were created by someone: the victims were made victims before they were made complicit.

Where all are guilty, no one is. If Arendt is right—and if her words have any applicability beyond the specific historical context in which she wrote—then my own jail-cell guilt trip was another form of phony sentimentality, in which I sought cover and refuge, some sort of perverse comfort, in a collective guilt spread so thin that it evaporates into air and disappears; an escape, in which I sought to be unburdened of the responsibility to judge, and of the responsibility such judgment would place on me.

The desire to be unburdened of judgment, and of responsibility, is pervasive. When the carbon lobby and its apologists, even in elite liberal institutions, argue that oil companies, their lobbyists, and the politicians who do their bidding are not to blame for global warming, but that all of us as consumers are guilty—that it's not, in other words, the oil barons and their craven servants who are guilty but "hypocritical" climate activists and struggling families everywhere, who rely on oil and gas to get to their jobs and to put food on their tables—it's as if apologists for Stalin blamed Soviet dissidents, and the average Soviet factory worker, for the horrors of Stalinism.

In fact, I would go further. What we are presented with now is chillingly reminiscent of the administrative, institutional, bureaucratic, and above all thoughtless criminality that so disturbed Hannah Arendt.

§

In a 1945 essay called "Organized Guilt and Universal Responsibility," Arendt articulated an insight that would later be developed to profound and provocative effect in *Eichmann in Jerusalem*. The Nazi system, she observes, "relies not on fanatics, nor on congenital murderers, nor on sadists; it relies entirely upon the normality of jobholders and family men." What its architects and managers, men like Himmler and Eichmann, discovered was that "for the sake of his pension, his life insurance, the security of his wife and children, such a man was ready to sacrifice his beliefs, his honor, and his human dignity." There was just one condition on which he insisted: "that he should be fully exempted from responsibility for his acts."

In her book on the Eichmann trial, Arendt describes this phenomenon as "the fearsome, word-and-thought-defying *banality of evil*." To be sure, our understanding of Eichmann and the surrounding history has improved in major ways since then, but the key issue Arendt raised—whether evil intent is required in order for evil to be done—is still very much with us. "The trouble with Eichmann," Arendt writes, "was precisely that so many were like him, and that the many were neither perverted nor sadistic, that they were, and still are, terribly and terrifyingly normal."

As we now know, thanks to the work of Bettina Stangneth in *Eichmann Before Jerusalem* (2011), Arendt (along with many others) was duped by Eichmann's performance in the courtroom. Based on Stangneth's research into previously unavailable material, we can say that Eichmann was a calculating, virulently antisemitic mass murderer, regardless of whether he killed anyone, or directly ordered anyone killed, himself. And yet, as Susan Neiman points out in her 2015 afterword to *Evil in Modern Thought* (2002), Arendt's central insight survives nevertheless, even if it doesn't apply to Eichmann himself. The truth about Eichmann "does not undermine [Arendt's] core idea that evil intentions are not required for evil actions," Neiman writes. In his courtroom performance, "Eichmann mimicked the thoughtless bureaucrats Germans now call desk-perpetrators, but they were there, in droves, to be mimicked—and without them, the intentions of men like Eichmann would seldom bear fruit."

Neiman argues for the relevance of Arendt's ideas about evil to our own situation, explicitly addressing climate catastrophe and the way it blurs the traditional lines between "natural" and "moral" evils. She goes on to write, "Our knowledge of how much evil can be done without intention makes the question of whether or not destruction and suffering were deliberate increasingly irrelevant. . . . Melting the Arctic? Bringing forth hurricanes? What boundaries remain?" Pointing to the reckless, even willful failure of government and industry to take the actions necessary to preserve a habitable planet, Neiman suggests that the terms in which Arendt spoke are entirely applicable. "When human heedlessness stokes destruction, then leaves the world's poorest people at its mercy, it isn't merely tragic; it's evil," she writes. "And nothing but the most banal of intentions is required for it to occur."

And yet the question remains why this matters to us now— whether the satisfactions of judging, smug or otherwise, sitting in a jail cell or in an armchair, are all we have left at this late hour.

4.

It was five days before the 2016 election when I got on a plane from Boston to Houston, then drove a midsized rental up Highway 59 to Nacogdoches in the piney woods of East Texas. A friend of mine, longtime pastor of a progressive, mostly white Baptist church there, had invited me to speak about climate justice at an interfaith conference on the state university campus. The theme of the conference, self-consciously topical, was "A Crisis of Empathy." The speakers and attendees were clergy, scholars, students, and laypeople of various Christian, Jewish, Muslim, Hindu, Buddhist, Native American, and other traditions, from all around East Texas and beyond.

The morning's keynote was by an aging Catholic priest from Louisville, Kentucky, soft-spoken, keenly intellectual, who'd spent decades opposing capital punishment and working with death row inmates alongside Sister Helen Prejean. A seasoned, gifted preacher, he knew how to pack an emotional punch, with compassion and vulnerability, and without self-righteousness. With empathy, you could say. And what he said that morning in the big modern lecture hall in Nacogdoches, and what has stuck with me (forgive me, Father, for I paraphrase), is that empathy, though much celebrated, is not always a reliable impulse toward moral action—that it can cut both ways. Because our natural inclination to empathize with the victims of crime and injustice, while generally a good thing, when mixed with our tribal instincts—our biases, conscious or not, in favor of people like ourselves, members of our own communities— can lead to a dehumanization of the stranger, the other, especially if that other is the perpetrator (or perceived to be) of a crime. It's easy to empathize with a victim, as one should; to empathize with a murderer—to see ourselves in another who violates our deepest values and taboos—is something else, something that may seem beyond our merely human capacity. Then he told the story of a death-row inmate with whom he'd grown close over the course of many years—a man guilty of his crime, who had accepted his guilt, who had sought forgiveness, a forgiveness that he knew could not undo what he had done, who had committed the rest of his life to helping others, and who went to his own murder with grace. The man had, to put it simply, repented, turned around. He had begun again.

The next morning, Saturday, I left Nacogdoches before dawn and drove up to Paris, the seat of Lamar County, where my dad was born and raised on small farms and in rural towns along the Missouri Pacific Railroad; where his great-grandparents had settled when they arrived from central Europe; and where his parents had farmed the blackland cotton as sharecroppers in the Depression, when he was a small child. But while my whole family on both sides is thoroughly Texan, I've never lived in Texas. I was born and grew up in the suburbs north of LA. Texas, for me, is the "old country."

I entered Paris on Highway 271, saw the Trump/Pence signs in the yards, saw the modern churches with their big parking lots, a billboard kindly offering "Concealed Hand Gun Training." A large, black pickup with tinted windows and a Confederate flag rode my tail.

My destination was Ward's Restaurant, a popular all-day diner on Clarksville Street. I sat at the horseshoe-shaped counter in the middle of the small, packed place and ordered a large Cowboy Omelet with hash browns, bacon, and biscuits and gravy. I settled in, ready to commune with the ancestral ghosts—all the God-fearing folks, poor, white, Christian, saved in Jesus yet lost in the church.

Straight across from me, on the other side of the counter, sat a white couple, quiet, unsmiling, early middle aged, maybe a few years younger than me and by the looks of it a good bit poorer. They were just sitting there—the man grizzled and mustached in a work shirt and camo cap, the woman plain and pretty in a gray sweat top—waiting uncomfortably for their food. They looked nice enough, just a little on edge, as though conscious of being stared at. I admit I was watching them (discreetly, I thought). For all I knew, we could have been kin. Or our fathers might have known each other, our grandmothers might have been friends, might have gone to church together, prayed together, sung the same hymns. And yet, who were they, this man and woman? Were they virulent racists? The white nationalist rank and file? Were they Christians, evangelical or otherwise? Were they churchgoers, or even religious at all? I had no idea—about any of it. No clue. Were they Trump voters? Were they going to vote? No idea. We never spoke. We exchanged glances, but not a word. All I knew then, and know now, is that they existed, they were human beings of a certain race and class. I had no way of knowing what they were guilty or not guilty of—if they were victims or executioners. Or neither. Or both.

§

"All I ask is that, in the midst of a murderous world, we agree to reflect on murder and to make a choice," writes Albert Camus in the 1946 essay "Neither Victims nor Executioners." Arendt admired Camus, liked him personally, perhaps because she saw in him not only a man of moral clarity but a man of action, one who had participated in the French Resistance.

In essays and lectures of the mid-to-late '60s and early '70s, Arendt tried to work out what it was, morally speaking, that was different about those who did not join or participate in a murderous system and who actively resisted the evil around them. In her lecture "Personal Responsibility Under Dictatorship," she offers that what we call conscience, by itself, is not enough—that it can lead to merely following, unthinkingly, the conventional moral standards and prevailing mores of one's society, even when, as demonstrated under Nazism and Stalinism, such standards have been turned upside down ("Thou shalt kill," "Thou shalt bear false witness," etc.). Instead, she finds, "the nonparticipants, called irresponsible by the majority, were the only ones who dared judge by themselves." These nonparticipants applied a different criterion, she writes: "They asked themselves to what extent they would still be able to live in peace with themselves after having committed certain deeds" and thus in some cases "chose to die when they were forced to participate." In other words, "they refused to murder, not so much because they still held fast to the command 'Thou shalt not kill,' but because they were unwilling to live together with a murderer—themselves."

Because it's in the nature of both totalitarian and nontotalitarian regimes to warp reality and turn conventional morality on its head, as seen in "the total moral collapse of respectable society during the Hitler regime," Arendt writes, the more reliable people "will be the doubters and skeptics . . . because they are used to examine [*sic*] things and to make up their own minds." Or as she puts it in a 1971 lecture: "The sad truth of the matter is that most evil is done by people who never made up their mind to be either bad or good."

The kind of thinking, of making up one's mind, that Arendt is talking about here, the internal dialogue with oneself that allows for questioning and judging, is a capacity shared by all, she goes on to suggest, not only an intellectual elite (who fail to exercise it as often as anyone, perhaps more). Nevertheless, such thinking "remains a marginal affair for society at large except in emergencies." At moments of crisis, she writes, "those who think are drawn out of hiding because their refusal to join is conspicuous and thereby becomes a kind of action."

This act of refusal, the refusal to join or to obey, the active withholding of consent and support, Arendt places among the forms of nonviolent resistance and civil disobedience developed to powerful effect in the twentieth century. Action, for Arendt, is humanity's highest calling and the essence of politics in the highest sense. Action is what we say and do in the public realm of human affairs, the realm in which history is shaped, initiative taken, in which we live as ourselves among others, in which we relate to each other not as abstractions but as distinct individuals, in the plural. "Action . . . corresponds to the human condition of plurality," Arendt writes in *The Human Condition* (1958), "to the fact that men, not Man, live on the earth and inhabit the world." This plurality, she writes, "is specifically *the* condition... of all political life."

But action itself, the capacity to initiate, to start something new, is rooted in something else, something even more basic, she tells us:

the mere fact of being born. For each birth marks something utterly unique, never before seen in the world, the beginning of a new and particular human life, with the unique potential it contains for action—that is, the perpetual capacity to begin again. "The life span of man running toward death would inevitably carry everything human to ruin and destruction," Arendt writes, "if it were not for the faculty of interrupting it and beginning something new, a faculty which is inherent in action like an ever-present reminder that men, though they must die, are not born in order to die but in order to begin."

Action, Arendt writes, is "the one miracle-working faculty of man."

§

In her report from the Jerusalem courtroom, Arendt relates the testimony of one Abba Kovner, described as a poet and author who had been a prominent member of the Jewish underground in Poland, and the story Kovner recounted, known to many of his listeners, of a German army sergeant named Anton Schmidt. It appears that Schmidt had led a patrol in Poland with the job of rounding up German soldiers separated from their units, and in the process he had come across and offered help to the Jewish underground by providing forged papers and the use of military trucks. Most importantly, Kovner told the court, "He did not do it for money."

"This had gone on for five months, from October, 1941, to March, 1942," Arendt writes, "when Anton Schmidt was arrested and executed."

As to why there were not more examples of Germans and Christian Poles helping the Jews, Arendt notes, "The risks were prohibitive; there was the story of an entire Polish family who had been executed in the most brutal manner because they had adopted a six-year-old Jewish girl." Such things were well known, so that in the brief time it took Kovner to describe Schmidt's actions, Arendt reports, "a hush settled over the courtroom; it was as though the crowd had spontaneously decided to observe the usual two minutes of silence in honor of the man named Anton Schmidt."

At which point, something strange and completely unexpected occurs in Arendt's courtroom narrative, a moment of hushed illumination. "And in those two minutes," she writes, "which were like a sudden burst of light in the midst of impenetrable, unfathomable darkness, a single thought stood out clearly, irrefutably, beyond question—how utterly different everything would be today . . . if only more such stories could have been told."

Those minutes and their hush seem to hang for an eternity over Arendt's text, and perhaps all of her work. "For the lesson of such stories," she tells us, "is simple and within everybody's grasp. Politically speaking, it is that under conditions of terror most people will comply but *some people will not.* . . . Humanly speaking, no more is required, and no more can reasonably be asked, for this planet to remain a place fit for human habitation."

5.

It's true that I told you there would be no comparisons, no historical analogies, only a genuine effort to understand, to learn, and yet I appear to have drawn just such an analogy after all.

Or have I, really? And if I have, what have we gained?

Totalitarian. . . . It will be objected that we're not living under a totalitarian system just yet, at least not in the literal sense, as conventionally understood. And that what we face is in no way similar, again speaking literally, to the Holocaust. True enough. But given what we now see, and what is coming, it's no longer an academic question what kind of a government we will have, what kind of a polity we will form, as we enter an era of increasing global instability, ripe for all the varieties of political and social evil. Because what else to call a system and ideology, carbon capitalism, seeking economic and political power over the earth at the expense of unimaginable numbers of lives, in which whole populations are rendered superfluous? A mindset that warps reality to its all-consuming ends, as if to prove that everything indeed is possible, that the very laws of physics, of nature, can be denied.

There are crimes against humanity the magnitude and cold brutality of which cannot be understood, cannot be weighed or calculated on any scale or spreadsheet—crimes, the motives for which are as commonplace, as banal, as quarterly earnings and political careers. Crimes that will be answered finally by the earth itself, when at last "omnipotent" humanity, or rather the heedless few, discover that while everything human, and much of the nonhuman, may be destroyed, not everything in the end is possible—regardless of what may or may not be permitted.

What I fear most is that these crimes kill even the desire for, and possibility of, birth—of new women and new men, born not to die but to begin.

And so the abyss opens—and it is all that I can do, perhaps all that can be reasonably asked, to hold on to what faith I have in what Hannah Arendt called the unsurpassable affirmation, that grace beyond reason, without which no amount of illumination can survive.

TWO

Carbon Ironies

The Moral Miscalculations
of Climate Fatalism

JUNE 2018

I've not yet given up believing both that the world ought to be better and that we have a duty to construct methods of improvement.
—William T. Vollmann, "Introduction," *Rising Up and Rising Down* (2004)

I did my arithmetic. . . . I threw up my hands.
—William T. Vollmann, "About Batteries and Fuel Cells," *Carbon Ideologies, Volume II: No Good Alternative* (2018)

Addressing an imagined reader in the all-too-likely "hot dark world" of our all-too-near human future, William T. Vollmann begins his two-volume, twelve-hundred-plus-page *Carbon Ideologies* with a curious and characteristically audacious gambit. In the opening pages of *Volume I: No Immediate Danger*, as he sets out upon this tome concerning fossil fuels and nuclear energy, Vollmann explains: "I do my best to look as will the future upon the

35

world in which I lived—namely, as surely, safely *vanished*. Nothing can be done to save it; therefore, nothing need be done. Hence this little book scrapes by without offering solutions. There were none; we had none."

Some twelve hundred pages later, near the end of *Volume II: No Good Alternative*—having heard from coal miners and refinery workers, oil executives and nuclear engineers, fracking enthusiasts and carbon lobbyists, politicians and industry-captured regulators, residents of variously poisoned communities, and even a few beleaguered activists—Vollmann beseeches his future reader to go easy on him and us. "If you could end up saying, 'Well, yes, we might have made the same mistakes as you, if we'd been lucky enough to live when you did,' I'd feel that *Carbon Ideologies* had accomplished some of its purpose," Vollmann writes. "How you judge us can mean nothing to us who are dead, but to *you* it might mean something, to accept that we were not all monsters; and forgiveness benefits the forgiver, so why wouldn't I prefer you to call our doings mistakes instead of crimes?" But Vollmann suspects this is a bit much to ask. "Most likely," he wearily admits, "you are a hard, angry person. . . . Beset by floods, droughts, diseases, and insect plagues . . . fearing for your children in the face of multiplying perils, how can you feel anything better than impatient contempt for my daughter and me, who lived so wastefully for our own pleasure?"

Now, perhaps this is unfair, but it occurs to me that Vollmann's imagined reader, sweating and hungry beside a dead, acidic ocean, may be entitled to ask why the author spent years of his comfortable (as he never tires of confessing), carbon-powered life writing a 1,200-page book about energy and global warming without offering more than a dismissive hand wave in the direction of "solutions" like solar, wind, geothermal, batteries, smart grids, etc.—at the very moment in history when such renewable energy technologies and their economics were beating all expectations. Well, it seems Mr. Vollmann simply doesn't believe there's anything we humans can do about a problem as big and complicated as climate change—after all, as a friendly pastor in West Virginia said to him, *the Earth is so large!* And even if there were, it would almost certainly require people like himself to engage politically and make some kind of sustained collective effort, which would be tedious and boring and difficult. And while it's possible that the logically fallacious (see tu quoque) obsession with his own carbon complicity and supposed "hypocrisy" may offer him a convenient excuse for not lifting a finger, it may also be the case that he simply doesn't want to look like the sentimental chump who falls for some hope-mongering twaddle about *fighting for humanity* and *not giving up on each other*, and all of that. Whatever the reason, he tells his misfortunate reader: "I am sorry."

I'm no Vollmannologist, no connoisseur of Vollmanniana, and thus unqualified to judge this book's place within the monumental Vollmann oeuvre—whether, for example, it deserves mention alongside his National Book Award–winning novel, *Europe Central* (2005)—so please don't consider this a serious assessment of its literary merits. I'll leave that to the experts. However, I do feel compelled to say that, as much as I may quibble with Vollmann's preordained conclusions about our climate future and attendant responsibilities, I quite *enjoyed* these volumes—he's a damn good writer!—and I heartily recommend nearly all twelve-hundred-some-odd pages to those who may actually have the time and inclination to read them.

One of the enjoyable things about this massive work is the way Vollmann employs irony, and that bluntest implement of irony called sarcasm, throughout the volumes. He can be quite humorous. You might even call this the *Infinite Jest* of climate books. Indeed, at some point deep into the weeds of *Carbon Ideologies*—perhaps a hundred and fifty pages into the first volume's two-hundred-page data- and table-filled "Primer" on our carbon-fueled industrial economy and lifestyles—I had to stop and ask myself whether Vollmann was not simply fucking with me (duh!), and whether I'd missed some grand joke and was gamely, gullibly soldiering on through his forest of tables with their technical definitions and calculations and the countless footnotes with their lengthy caveats and sharp asides and erudite literary-historical citations. (Perhaps a small sampling from the primer's table of contents will convey the texture of this book's computational adventures: "Power Wastage by Group-Driven Machine Tools, *ca.* 1945 . . . Power Wastage During Machining Operations at an Unspecified Toyota Factory, *ca.* 2000 . . . Power Wastage by Devices in Standby Mode, 2000–2010 . . . Per Capita Power Consumption, *ca.* 1925 and *ca.* 2014, *in multiples of the 1925 Japanese average* . . . Carbon Dioxide Emissions from Fuel Consumption, World and Selected Countries, 1971 and 2004, *in multiples of the US percentage increase over that period* . . . Power Generation's Share of Greenhouse Gas Emissions for Selected Countries, 2007–2014, *in multiples of the 2012 European Union value. . .*" et cetera ad absurdum. You get the picture.)

Surely, I said to myself, Vollmann is not so cynical as to make an elaborate literary entertainment, a kind of ironic parlor game, out of the greatest human catastrophe of all time.

Well, no, not exactly. With some relief, I came to realize that for all the darkly comic ironies and over-the-top absurdities, Vollmann was actually engaged in an earnest work of documentary reportage—with many of his own striking photographs to accompany the text—having traveled from the radioactive environs of Fukushima, Japan, to the oil-soaked towns of Oklahoma, the coal fields of West Virginia and Bangladesh, the fracked plains of Colorado, and the

Persian Gulf refineries and migrant worker camps of Dubai, interviewing people of all classes and degrees of complicity at this precipice moment for human civilization. This is the longest and nerdiest book about climate and energy I've ever read (and trust me, I've read a few), as well as the most useless (as Vollmann would no doubt admit), but in truth there's something admirable, even noble, about the sheer amount of time and effort—and the sheer *humanity*—that went into these volumes. (Personally, as one whose own father worked as a roughneck in the West Texas oil patch putting himself through a small Christian college in the late 1940s, I have sincere respect for the way Vollmann genuinely and empathetically humanizes his subjects, warts—to put it kindly—and all.)

And yet, for all that I find enjoyable and admirable in Vollmann's project, I'm also sharply opposed to his brand of climate fatalism, which seems to be symptomatic, a kind of irresistible temptation, among intellectuals and other expensively educated types these days—admirers of Roy Scranton's *Learning to Die in the Anthropocene*, for example, or *The New Yorker* essays of Jonathan Franzen. And it's this sense of utter futility and resignation in the face of our human emergency which would seem to warrant a reply. Because Vollmann is correct on some important level, but only up to a point. To borrow the phrase he used in *Rising Up and Rising Down* (2003), his seven-volume moral treatise on violence—which, along with *Poor People* (2007), he considers a companion to *Carbon Ideologies*—his "moral calculus" here is fundamentally flawed, based as it is on a common misunderstanding or mischaracterization of the climate catastrophe.

§

Climate change has a way of bringing out the moralist in the most hardened cynic and the most complacent fatalist (believe me, friends, I have some experience in this area), so it should be no surprise that Vollmann—who, after all, is the author of the afore-mentioned seven-volume treatise—is concerned with the moral quandaries and complexities of our planetary predicament. In fact, there's even a section of *Rising Up and Rising Down*, referenced in *Carbon Ideologies*, in which he considers the possible justifications for violence in "defense of the Earth." (It's complicated.)

And there's a good bit that Vollmann gets right, or so it seems to me, in terms of the moral calculus on climate. This is especially the case in his vivid, often affecting, unerringly humane portraits of ordinary people caught up in the carbon system—and nowhere more so than in West Virginia, where the people he meets, at all social levels, have been literally poisoned by that system, indoctrinated and deceived by its ideologues, sacrificed on the altar of limitless profits and the so-called patriotic duty to "keep the lights on." He knows there's no moral equivalence between these folks and the executives, lobbyists, politicians, and revolving-door regulators who do everything in their considerable power—including pitiful appeals to victimhood—to keep the system humming along. So it's satisfying when he drops all sarcasm near the end of the book and lays it on the line:

> Those who found themselves compelled by economics to be complicit in the production, distribution, and consumption of harmful energies . . . were not especially at fault. For them, fossil fuels constituted sheer subsistence. . . . Even less could I accuse those who had not been educated to understand the almost invisibly approaching misery.
>
> However, I began to believe that those who selfishly, maliciously or with gross negligence did harm ought to be singled out, shamed and maybe even . . . punished.—What

constituted gross negligence? A parent who left a loaded gun in reach of a baby was surely responsible for the result. Those West Virginia officials, Colorado lobbyists, and Oklahoma Chamber of Commerce types who publicly advanced the agendas of their chosen fossil fuels but refused to even acknowledge questions about global warming stood convicted, in my mind at least, of authoritarian partisanship. I would have heard their side; they were not even willing to *tell me* theirs, much less ask about mine. And they had power. . . . *These* are the ones, my friend. These are the ones who laid you low.

Given such exemplary moral clarity, I found it puzzling that Vollmann let one of his most important interviewees, former ConocoPhillips CEO Archie Dunham, entirely off the hook, failing to mention that Dunham—though apparently a very warm and courteous man who welcomed Vollmann into his home overlooking the Pacific Ocean—served as a director of the American Petroleum Institute. The API, if you don't know, is one of the principal arms of the carbon lobby and the decades-long campaign to mislead the public on climate science and obstruct any useful policies to rein in emissions. At the very least, it would seem that Mr. Dunham, no doubt a very nice person, was a willing accessory or onlooker to these unprecedented political crimes against humanity.

Nevertheless, for a writer so finely attuned to the nuances of moral reasoning, Vollmann displays a surprisingly simplistic and binary view of the climate situation.

Yes, of course, we're fucked. (Though it's important to specify the "we" in this formulation, because the global poor, the disenfranchised, the very young, and the yet-to-be-born are certifiably *far more fucked* than such affluent, white, middle-aged male Americans as Vollmann and myself.) But here's the thing: with climate change as with so much else, *all fuckedness is relative*. Climate catastrophe, at this stage, is not a binary *win* or *lose*, *solution* or *no-solution, fucked* or *not-fucked* situation. Just *how fucked* we/they will be—that is, what kind of civilization, or any sort of social justice, will be possible in the coming centuries or decades—depends on many things, including all sorts of historic, built-in systemic injustices we know all too well, and any number of contingencies we can't foresee. But most of all it depends on *what we do right now*, in our lifetimes. And by that I mean what we do *politically*, not only on climate but across the board, because large-scale political action—the kind that moves whole countries and economies in ways commensurate with the scale and urgency of the situation—has always been the only thing that matters here. (I really don't care about Vollmann's personal carbon footprint, or yours. I mean, please do try to lower it, because that's a good thing to do, but fussing and guilt-tripping over one's *individual* contribution to climate change is neither an intellectually nor a morally serious response to a *global systemic crisis*. That this still needs to be said at this late date is, to say the least, somewhat disappointing.)

As experts (and other people, like me) have been saying for years now, it is almost certainly too late to prevent highly disruptive and, in many places, catastrophic climate change within this century, with all the human misery and death that will bring. But it's also the case that rigorous analyses (though you won't find them in *Carbon Ideologies*), like those of Mark Jacobson and his colleagues at Stanford University, show how most of the world's energy systems could in fact be radically decarbonized in the coming decades; that the barriers are not technological or economic; and that there are now signs of the political and economic winds shifting globally, in spite of (and in response to) Donald Trump's election. Are they shifting fast enough? Not even close. Is the carbon lobby still doing everything it can to obstruct and delay? Yes, by all means. And even if the world somehow miraculously moves as fast as possible between now and midcentury, as scientists are calling for, will it *prevent* dangerous and destabilizing climate disruption for centuries and possibly millennia to come? Probably not. In fact, achieving the vaunted Paris Agreement goals would actually require "negative emissions" technologies, capable of pulling carbon dioxide out of the atmosphere on a vast scale, which remain largely speculative (not to say fantasy).

So, yes, Vollmann and other doomists are right that it's a no-win situation—depending on what you mean by "win." If you mean "stopping" or "solving" climate change and preserving the world as we've known it, then the climate fight was "lost" a long time ago, maybe before it began. And yet science also tells us that, even at this late date, some versions of "losing" could look far worse than others. *We can still lose less badly!* Not the most inspiring battle cry, perhaps, but when you understand the stakes—human survival—still a cause worth lifting a finger for.

Scientists don't really know with precision (which means William T. Vollmann doesn't really know) where the atmospheric tipping points actually are, and whether we've already crossed some of them or soon will—see, for example, the accelerating collapse of Arctic sea ice and the melting permafrost—making some worst-case scenarios unstoppable. Climate experts will tell you that every fraction of a degree of warming we prevent could be well worth the effort. So is it too late to prevent many catastrophic impacts across much of the world? Almost certainly. Is it too late to prevent the worst-case scenarios and thus *even greater suffering of billions more human beings?* Maybe. Maybe not. We don't know. And that's the point. As for the politics, maybe the obstacles really are insurmountable. *But maybe they're not.* History shows that revolutionary change, both political and technological, is almost never foreseen—or even believed possible—by those living in the historical moment. Again, that's the point. We *don't know* exactly when it will be "too late" (too late for *what?* we should always ask), or what may be possible if we keep pushing hard enough.

If, in the face of this kind of uncertainty, you're comfortable throwing up your hands and doing nothing, very well; it's your choice. Vollmann won't think any less of you, and quite honestly, neither will I. Political action, sustained commitment, sacrifice— these are a lot to ask of anyone. But please don't take moral comfort from assurances that there is nothing to be done. There's plenty.

Which is one reason it's too bad that Vollmann, though he does profile a few seemingly isolated activists fighting the "Carbon Goliaths" in West Virginia and Colorado and Bangladesh, never acknowledges the existence of the global grassroots climate movement that has become a serious force over the past decade. In case you're unaware, this is the bottom-up movement that has not only stopped, in the US alone, fossil-fuel megaprojects like the Keystone XL pipeline, Pacific Northwest coal export terminals, and regional fracked-gas infrastructure in the Northeast, with thousands of ordinary citizens putting their bodies on the line—and hundreds of thousands coming into the streets—to do so. It's also the movement that's pushed global institutions with more than six trillion dollars in assets to divest from the fossil-fuel industry, fundamentally altering the conversation on climate and carbon— bringing concepts like "stranded assets" and "carbon bubble" into the mainstream (but not into the pages of *Carbon Ideologies*)—putting the industry's political culpability and its criminally reckless business model front and center, even beginning to hurt its bottom line. These are no small accomplishments.

But there's plenty to be done, too, for those who can't see themselves as climate activists—because the basic political struggles for democracy and human rights, in this country and around the world, are as central to our climate future as the fights to keep carbon in the ground. For those who must try to adapt and live through what's coming—including Vollmann's daughter and my own kids—there won't be any climate justice, or any justice at all, no matter what the global temperature may be, if we lose our democracy.

Unfortunately, many of the sort of educated, literate folks Vollmann is writing for don't seem to understand all this. Or maybe they don't want to understand. Perhaps they prefer to look away. It's so much easier to tell oneself the game is up, that nothing can be done, that nothing ever could have been done, so why bother? It's perversely comforting to wallow in tragic-ironic guilt over one's carbon complicity—doing nothing.

The fact that there's no moral purity and no "solution" (a word that should be struck from the climate lexicon) in the simplistic binary sense doesn't mean that nothing can or should be done, even at this late date, even in the face of catastrophe on some unknowable schedule and scale—*especially* if you care at all about your fellow human inhabitants of this planet, as William T. Vollmann, to his great credit, most clearly and unironically does. If nothing else, just holding on to our humanity as we sweat in the dark ought to keep us busy.

THREE

Living in Truth

The Green New Deal
and the Revolution We Need

APRIL 2019

The year was 1989, the month was November, and I was a twenty-one-year-old senior at a New England college, when one day in my dorm's cavernous wood-paneled dining hall—I'll never forget this—a classmate stood on a chair and announced excitedly to the room that the Berlin Wall was coming down.

And so it was; we watched it on TV. The Eastern Bloc disintegrated before our eyes, as though miraculously, and more or less without a shot. "A political earthquake was shattering the frozen topography of post-World War II Europe," Tony Judt later wrote of those events in *Postwar: A History of Europe Since 1945* (2005). "What had once seemed permanent and somehow inevitable would take on a more transient air." In a mere two years' time, the Soviet Union itself ceased to exist, and the Cold War nightmare, the only global political reality we'd ever known, was over.

Those revolutions of 1989 were complex events, and there's surely no single explanation of why they happened precisely when and how they did. But in a justly famous samizdat essay titled "The Power of the Powerless" (1978), the dissident Czech playwright

47

Václav Havel—among the leaders of Prague's Velvet Revolution
that November and December and the first president of the newly
democratic Czechoslovakia—argued that the most potent form
of resistance to the Soviet Bloc system was what he called "living
within the truth." He writes: "Because the regime is captive to its
own lies, it must falsify everything. It falsifies the past. It falsifies
the present, and it falsifies the future. . . . It pretends to respect
human rights. . . . It pretends to pretend nothing." For the system
to function and to maintain its control of society, Havel goes on,
"Individuals need not believe all these mystifications, but they must
behave as though they did, or they must at least tolerate them in
silence, or get along well with those who work with them. For this
reason, however, they must *live within a lie*."

To illustrate, Havel conjures a hypothetical greengrocer who
decides he can no longer live in such a way. One day, Havel writes,
"something in our greengrocer snaps. . . . He begins to say what he
really thinks at political meetings. And he even finds the strength
in himself to express solidarity with those whom his conscience
commands him to support." In taking this step, the greengrocer
"rejects the ritual and breaks the rules of the game. . . . His revolt is an attempt to *live within the truth*." For Havel, the effect of
such simple acts is radically revelatory: his greengrocer "has broken
through the exalted façade of the system and exposed the real, base
foundations of power." This is "extremely dangerous," Havel notes,
not just for the greengrocer (as Havel, who went to prison in 1979,
well knew) but for the regime, the system itself. In that essay Havel
goes on, prophetically, to describe the "singular, explosive, incalculable political power of living within the truth."

As a twenty-one-year-old, I had yet to read any Václav Havel
(though his plays and essays were available in English), but it didn't
matter—it was clear enough what was happening. History, far from

ending, had been jolted to life by the explosive, incalculable power of those hundreds of thousands filling the streets and city squares. My fellow American students and I were witnesses, from across an ocean, to the kind of fundamental, world-changing political action that Hannah Arendt, so inspired by the 1956 Hungarian uprising, called "the one miracle-working faculty of man." We literally came of age as witnesses to revolution.

§

As riveting as those scenes were, the revolutions in Eastern Europe and the unimaginable collapse of the Soviet Union were not the only world-altering processes unfolding on planet Earth as my generational cohort came of age. There was also a "digital revolution" underway, and many of us would soon be swept up in it, building websites and "going online." At the same time, and with far less hype, we were the generation coming of age with the increasing awareness of global warming—and, like most everyone else around us, doing little or nothing about it.

Indeed that very fall, in September 1989, there arrived a book called *The End of Nature* by a young *New Yorker* writer named Bill McKibben, who reported and meditated upon the well-advanced science of the greenhouse effect. The year before, NASA climatologist James Hansen had testified to Congress that global warming was in fact happening, as long predicted, as a result of greenhouse gas emissions, mainly from fossil fuels. (This was no surprise to scientists and executives at Exxon and other big oil companies, who were already well aware of their products' effects on the atmosphere and the likely disastrous consequences.) McKibben's book was a probing extended essay on the deeper meaning of it all, in which he announced the arrival of what today we call the Anthropocene.

Three decades and a shelf full of subsequent books since that first warning, and after more than a decade of relentless and increasingly consequential grassroots movement-building as founder of 350.org—fundamentally changing the conversation on climate and the fossil-fuel industry—McKibben brings us *Falter: Has the Human Game Begun to Play Itself Out?* And in its pages he argues convincingly that the unstoppable momentum of climate change, along with exponential and uncontrolled technological leaps in artificial intelligence and genetic engineering, represent possibly insurmountable threats to humanity and what it means to be human. The book affirms McKibben as among a very few of our most compelling truth tellers about the climate catastrophe *and* the ideological forces driving it—most notably, in his account, the hyperindividualist, Ayn Randian libertarianism of the Kochs and their fellow free-market true believers, not least in Silicon Valley.

And among the stark truths McKibben tells in his new book is that the Kochs and their carbon-lobby friends, given their successful decades-long strategy of deceit, obstruction, and "predatory delay" (Alex Steffen's phrase), have essentially won. That is, the "climate fight" as we've known it—the struggle to prevent "catastrophic" global warming (by any *humane* definition) and preserve some semblance of the planet humanity has always known—is lost. The fight now is for nothing less than human survival—while at the same time, and equally important, we struggle to hold on to our humanity.

Not that anyone who's paid attention to McKibben's writing and speaking for the past decade—or three—should be shocked. Here's McKibben in *The End of Nature* on what the science was already telling us in 1989: "Now it is too late—not too late to ameliorate some of the changes and so perhaps to avoid the most gruesome of their consequences. But the scientists agree that we have already pumped enough gas into the air so that a significant rise in temperature and a subsequent shift in weather are inevitable."

"For many years," McKibben told me in a 2013 interview (quoted at length in my 2015 book about the climate movement), "I have been very insistent on saying to people that stopping global warming is no longer one of the options. We can keep it from getting worse than it would otherwise get—and the difference between a world where the temperature has gone up two degrees [Celsius], and a world where it's gone up four degrees, is a difference very much worth fighting for. It might prove to be the difference between a world with civilization and a world without it." Even then, scientists were telling us that warming of two degrees—a virtual certainty absent radical global action—would likely be devastating for most of humanity, starting with the poorest and most marginalized, and that a business-as-usual trajectory could well lead to an uninhabitable planet. (Mainstream coverage of David Wallace-Wells's *The Uninhabitable Earth* suggests a new interest in these dire scenarios among liberal media elites. But as Wallace-Wells notes, they're far from news.)

"You can't really, plausibly, give an 'I have a dream' speech for climate change," McKibben told me back then, "because the two possibilities are a miserable century and an impossible one."

You see, Bill McKibben was a climate doomist (or "doomer," if you're old school) before "doomism" was cool. But being a doomist—that is, by my definition, accepting the fact that almost any possible future now involves catastrophic levels of climate change—is not the same as being a fatalist (much less a nihilist, as some, who don't seem to know what nihilism is, would have it). Because McKibben has also been telling us that there's a range of possible climate futures, along with a range of possible *social* futures that will determine how and whether we prepare for and *live through* what's coming. How hot and chaotic it gets within this century—and how democratic or antidemocratic, how just or unjust, the response—will depend on the choices humanity makes *right now*. Most of all, the *big political choices*, the kind that can radically shift economies and societies around the world. In other words, as McKibben and many others, including Naomi Klein (and, yes, myself), have been arguing for years—taking a cue from Indigenous, Black, brown, and other frontline-community leaders (see, for example, the Climate Justice Alliance)—it will depend more than anything on our social movements and how hard we're willing to struggle, together and for the long haul, against those obstructing and delaying any sane and equitable path forward. And not simply against the carbon lobbyists and their corporate masters, or the science-denying politicians who feed at their trough, but also those across the political spectrum—and within the Democratic Party—whose power and status depend upon the willingness of many to *live within a lie*.

The lies that one may choose to live within, and upon which the carbon regime rests, come in various forms: whether it's the falsehood that we're simply "fucked" and there's "nothing left to be done," as we've seen with the fatalists; or, on the flip side, that we can still "solve the climate crisis" with incremental market-friendly measures (a modest carbon tax, say) that won't interfere with profits and growth; or that fracked gas can be a "bridge fuel" into the distant future; or that "climate denial" is only a problem on the political right and not pervasive in its various forms among so-called pragmatic moderates and greenwashing center-left elites; or that deep decarbonization will ever be politically possible without a commitment to economic and racial justice; or, perhaps most insidious, that "we"—everyone, even our children, by virtue of being human—"are all to blame" for the failure to address the crisis, as if big-money political obstruction and predatory delay are not willful crimes against humanity. (As Arendt put it, "Where all are guilty, no one is.")

But at this late date, maybe the most damaging lie we tell ourselves is this: that the climate catastrophe can ever be seriously addressed within the corporate-owned and -operated political system, the mockery of democracy, under which we live; that business and politics and even activism *as usual* can continue if we want any chance of a livable—to say nothing of a just—human future.

§

In his preface to *Falter*, which he calls "An Opening Note on Hope," McKibben tells us: "A writer doesn't owe a reader hope—the only obligation is honesty—but I want those who pick up this volume to know that its author lives in a state of engagement, not despair."

It's a sincere and inspiring statement, the kind I've come to expect from my friend Bill McKibben. The question is: What do honesty and engagement require of us—those of us privileged enough to be having this conversation—now?

"Perhaps our electoral systems are strong enough to reverse the craziness," McKibben writes in *Falter*, having just given us a tour de force indictment of how the Kochs and their ideological fellow travelers achieved such outsized leverage over our politics. On the other hand, not to let establishment liberals off the hook, he acknowledges, "Perhaps the power of money in our political life is so great that it will require something that looks more like a nonviolent revolution."

McKibben's purpose in the book is not to sketch the contours of such a revolution, but I wish he'd said a bit more about the nature of the radical political change necessary at this point—the kind of change the resistance he calls for must bring about if we're to have a

chance. Because given what science is telling us about our accelera-
tion toward climate catastrophe and what that means for humanity's
future, together with the facts McKibben lays out about our political system's failure to respond, it feels increasingly like something
fundamental has shifted, that the nature of the climate struggle itself has irreversibly changed—that if the "old" fight is lost, then the
"new" fight (if we can even call it new) is of a wholly different order.
But how does one build a movement powerful enough to meet the
challenge if one isn't clear about the nature of the challenge?

Because the challenge now is nothing less than transforming
the global economy and winding down the wealthiest, most powerful, and most ruthless industry on Earth—one that effectively owns
and controls our political system—within the next decade or two.
Recall that the IPCC's major report in October 2018 concluded
that holding warming near 1.5 degrees Celsius—thus preventing
hundreds of millions of deaths and social chaos and conflict on an
unprecedented scale—requires cutting *global* greenhouse emissions
by roughly *50 percent* by 2030 and *eliminating* them by midcentury, together with the massive deployment of "negative emissions"
technologies that are unproven at anything like the necessary scale.
Even with the assurance of experts that the global transformation
required is technologically and economically feasible, the idea that
it's still *politically* possible to avert two degrees Celsius of warming—
much less 1.5—if progressive Democrats in this country simply organize more effectively and elect the right candidates, borders on
utopian fantasy. Politics and activism as usual have failed—global
annual emissions, of which the United States now accounts for about
15 percent, are rising, not falling—and it defies reason to think that
more of the same will save us.

As one who has now given more than a few years of my life
to the climate struggle, this is not easy to say, and yet honesty

requires it. In the face of these dire scientific and political realities, the *climate movement*'s time has passed. That is, the movement that McKibben and countless others have spent the past decade and more building—bringing many hundreds of thousands into the streets, inspiring thousands of acts of civil disobedience, giving rise to a new generation of young activists demanding climate justice—is no longer sufficient, if it ever was. It's been clear for some time now, since well before Trump's election—around the time Barack Obama and the Democratic Party sold out to the carbon lobby with an "all of the above" energy policy that made the United States the world's largest producer of oil and gas—that a social and political movement built primarily around climate change, per se, or even the concept of climate and environmental justice, will not build enough power *on its own* to break the death grip of corporations and private wealth on our political system. At least, not in the time we have. The sheer depth, scale, and speed of the changes required at this point are beyond anything a mere "climate movement" can possibly accomplish.

The pretense that anything less than revolutionary political change is now required amounts to a form of denial. This is not to say that climate activists should simply stop what they're doing and go join "the revolution." (Well, maybe some of us should.) We still need action *at all levels* to keep carbon in the ground—all of those fights are vital; indeed they are part of the revolution we need. And yet climate activists have no choice, at this late date, but to approach this work differently, to understand it differently, not merely as "climate action" but as part of something larger, more fundamental, more radical—a broad, nonviolent revolutionary movement for democracy and human rights.

This is why the vision of a comprehensive Green New Deal put forward by Representative Alexandria Ocasio-Cortez, Senator

Edward Markey, and their young allies Justice Democrats and the Sunrise Movement, is such a welcome development. Its aims, which include fully decarbonizing the US economy, putting the fossil-fuel industry out of business in this country within a mere decade or two—while at the same time putting jobs, health care, and racial justice at the center of the GND's ten-year national mobilization— are, in fact, revolutionary. And those pushing for it, especially the young people whose literal lives are on the line, need to own this. If the Green New Deal is to be as transformative as we know is neces- sary, then it must be more than just another legislative policy agenda for the Democratic Party. It needs to be among the central rallying points for a revolutionary democracy movement, or "movement of movements"—with principles of climate and environmental justice at the core—into which the various strands of the climate movement fold themselves as one part, or rather, many interwoven parts.

Otherwise the proverbial cart—transformative policy—is before the horse: transformative democratic power. The revolutionary aims of a comprehensive Green New Deal require a democratic revolution.

Given how far we are from realizing such a vision—despite the insurgent energy and promise of "political revolution" propelling Bernie Sanders's presidential campaign—all of this might under- standably induce the despair of which McKibben writes. And yet, even if such a transformative democracy movement is unlikely to succeed within the short time frame we have—even if it is too late to prevent runaway warming and some sort of global collapse—it will still be worth fighting and sacrificing for, even, I believe, dying for. As it always has been. Because the only thing more horrific than runaway climate catastrophe is the very real prospect of living into it, within mere decades, under a racist, nationalist, militarized, oligarchic political system that is leading us toward, if it hasn't al- ready become, an authoritarian police state. *The only thing worse than climate catastrophe is climate catastrophe* plus *fascism.*

Yes, talk of "revolution," and not as a mere metaphor, tends to scare people, including people on the left, and understandably so. And it makes the cynics and the fatalists and the Very Serious types roll their eyes. Granted, it can be difficult to imagine such a revolutionary mass movement in this country right now.

Unless, that is, one can imagine a movement that looks like the sum of the grassroots mobilizations we've already seen on the left in recent years. Unless, in other words, one can imagine Standing Rock and Black Lives Matter, the Poor People's Campaign and the People's Climate March, Occupy and the Fight for $15, the Women's March and the March for Our Lives, Sanctuary Cities and Moral Mondays, #NoKXL and #NoBanNoWall and #AbolishICE. Imagine all of these—and more—not as separate issues and campaigns but one massive solidarity movement; and not as a series of one-off events but a strategic, sustained, disruptive, nonviolent mass mobilization to bring business and politics as usual to a halt in this country—by means of large-scale and widespread direct action, general strikes, and noncooperation, taking and occupying public spaces, and a willingness for genuine sacrifice—in order to force a confrontation with the American political system that cannot be ignored or co-opted; to force a reckoning. In other words, unless one can imagine an authentic struggle for democracy, the makings of which already exist.

§

Shortly after the election of Donald Trump in November 2016, McKibben delivered The Nation Institute's inaugural Jonathan Schell Memorial Lecture. In that lecture, McKibben points to Schell's 2003 book, *The Unconquerable World*, about the potential of (mostly) nonviolent social movements to bring revolutionary change—from independence in India to civil rights in the United States to ending apartheid in South Africa and, yes, the Eastern European revolutions of 1989. It's a book and a theme to which McKibben returns in the final chapters of *Falter*, quoting Schell's memorable formulation: "Violence is the method by which the ruthless few can subdue the passive many. Nonviolence is a means by which the active many can overcome the ruthless few."

The point of nonviolent resistance, McKibben argues, and of the social movements it grows from and strengthens, is less about passing specific legislation than "changing the zeitgeist." Once that happens, electoral and/or legislative victory—even political and social revolution—can rapidly follow. And so McKibben ended his Schell lecture with a promise that "movement-building—the mobilization of large numbers of people, and of deep passion, through the employment of all the tools at a nonviolent activist's disposal—will continue, though it moves onto very uncertain ground with our new political reality."

Of course, nothing is apt to change if we stay in our single-issue silos or try to impose strict ideological uniformity across an entire movement of movements. As Václav Havel argued, rather than loyalty to abstract ideas and doctrines, we need more than anything loyalty to one another as human beings.

In his 1984 essay "Politics and Conscience," published not long after he was released from prison, Havel pointed to what he believed are the most powerful tools of nonviolent resistance, the means by which we hold on to our humanity in dark times. "We must not be ashamed that we are capable of love, friendship, solidarity, sympathy, and tolerance," he writes, "but just the opposite: we must set these fundamental dimensions of our humanity free from their 'private' exile and accept them as the only genuine starting point of meaningful human community."

Fine words, but not worth much, as Havel knew, if words were all they remained. And so he points to what he sees "becoming evident" in the world: namely, that explosive, incalculable power of a "seemingly powerless person who dares to cry out the word of truth and to stand behind it with all his person and all his life, ready to pay a high price"—that is, the power of living within the truth.

§

Postscript: In April 2020, I posted the following letter, in slightly different form, to my friends and comrades in the US climate-justice movement:

"Yes" Is Not Enough

Dear friends,

As I write, it is six weeks since everything changed where I live, in eastern Massachusetts, when the schools closed and businesses began sending their employees home.

As we're all too aware, this week of April was set to be a major moment for our swelling movement in the midst of this most consequential election year—what might have been our most important mobilization as a movement to date, building on the historic surge of momentum since 2018, when the Green New Deal exploded onto the national stage. And yet here we are, faced with this fearful, disorienting new reality.

Like anyone else who's written and agitated on climate and climate justice for the past decade or more, I've always known that we'd have to keep working in the face of adversity and increasing instability in the coming years—but I'll admit that I never anticipated anything so sudden and near-totally immobilizing as this.

Because let's face it, despite our best digital efforts, the coronavirus has all but taken us out of action—even as the fossil-fuel industry and its political servants exploit the crisis, doubling down on brazen climate destruction under cover of the pandemic.

It has to be said: This all-consuming health and economic emergency is the most dangerous and uncertain moment we have ever faced as a movement. There's a real anxiety among many of us, a sense that all the hard-won momentum, all the power that's been built—as seen in the unprecedented Green New Deal coalition that helped power the transformative Bernie Sanders campaign and forced climate justice into the national debate—is in danger of stalling and ebbing away.

As a movement, we face a moment of decision. When the pandemic crisis recedes, as it eventually will, we can choose to fall in line with a corporate-political establishment, including the Democratic Party, that wants nothing more than a "return to normalcy" and politics as usual—in which the fossil-fuel industry is rescued and the climate emergency is again relegated to second- or third-tier priority, at best. Or we can refuse to go along, remove our consent—and recommit to an escalated and intensified nonviolent struggle.

The movement of movements we've been building for over a decade is led, conspicuously, by young people, some of whom I've known and worked alongside for years, and by Indigenous and frontline climate-justice groups for whom walking away is not an option and climate justice not an abstract concept. For a decade and more, many of these leaders and organizers, of all ages and circumstances, have been throwing themselves into the fights against fossil-fuel extraction and infrastructure—tar sands, fracking, oil refineries, coal plants—and into the global campaign for fossil-fuel divestment, signaling to financial markets that carbon reserves are stranded assets and fossil-fuel companies are the walking dead.

It seems safe to say that there would be no movement today for a Green New Deal had these fights of the past decade not taken place—if many thousands, young and old, had not been willing to confront the fossil-fuel industry, put their bodies on the line, and commit themselves to building a genuine nonviolent resistance demanding a just transition to a green and democratic economy. If anyone wants to know where the Green New Deal came from, tell them it was born of resistance. Tell them to ask Alexandria Ocasio-Cortez, who was galvanized at Standing Rock.

Now, just as we've begun to feel and flex our power, we find ourselves unable to mobilize—that is, actually mobilize, together, physically, in the streets and on campuses, on the pipeline routes and railroad tracks, in the bank offices and halls of government, all the places where we cannot be ignored. There are some things we can do digitally, of course, but we all know a hashtag echo chamber offers little resistance to a ruthless industry and the political system that props it up.

And in this state of suspension—and, frankly, fear—as we approach the November election and (whatever may happen) try to think beyond it, there may be an impulse to let resistance slide, and to focus on the economic and public health agenda of the Green New Deal, with its positive message of jobs, clean energy, universal health care, and education. And of course this inspiring and reality-based vision is essential, especially in an election year when the stakes are no less than democracy and Earth's climate itself. Indeed, that's the political promise of the Green New Deal—the way it offers an affirming, broadly appealing agenda to organize around, the way it meets the vast majority of Americans where they are, addressing their daily needs, in terms of economic, social, and environmental justice. To all of these, it offers a resounding yes.

But in the struggle for a livable world—and "it must be a

struggle" (Frederick Douglass)—in the face of the entrenched forces lined up against us, all the organizing and advocacy our movement can muster on behalf of this positive vision, while absolutely necessary, will never be sufficient. Indeed, precisely because of this pandemic and economic collapse, our collective nonviolent resistance to the fossil fuel industry, its financial backers, and its political allies, in both parties, is more important than ever. To win anything like a Green New Deal, "Yes" will never be enough.

In her influential 2017 book *No Is Not Enough*, written in the immediate wake of Trump's election, Naomi Klein made the compelling argument (building on 2014's *This Changes Everything*) that to confront our political and climate crises together requires that positive vision, that "Yes," and not only resistance. "We have to tell a different story," she wrote, one that offers "a plan for the future that is credible and captivating enough that a great many people will fight to see it realized, no matter the shocks and scare tactics thrown their way." Drawing from her experience as an instigator and coauthor of the popular Leap Manifesto program in Canada, the northern precursor to our Green New Deal, this argument has become a kind of gospel for younger Green New Dealers to whom Klein, as Bill McKibben has noted, is something of an "intellectual godmother."

But Naomi never argued that our movement of movements can afford to relegate resistance to the back burner. Quite the opposite. In that same book she argued, as she has long argued, that recognizing the necessity of a positive agenda "doesn't mean that resisting the very specific attacks—on families, on people's bodies, on communities, on individual rights—is suddenly optional. There is no choice but to resist." It has never been an either/or. Both "yes" and "no" are equally necessary—not only morally, I would add, but strategically. It would be a historic mistake for the Green New Deal movement to deemphasize or retreat from the kind of escalated nonviolent resistance we've seen in the past. After all, it was the Sunrise Movement's large civil disobedience action, their occupation of Nancy Pelosi's Capitol Hill office, that forced the GND into the national conversation—and we know that far more direct and disruptive action is possible.

Clearly, a pandemic is not the time for fossil-fuel resisters to be filling the jails—which would recklessly endanger our own and others' lives. But this is also not the time to lose resolve and give up on nonviolent resistance as a strategic tool. Electoral organizing around the Green New Deal vision is, of course, essential—and, at the same time, it's imperative to prepare now for an intensified nonviolent struggle against the fossil-fuel industry and our corporate-controlled political system when the pandemic recedes.

To be sure, there's already a sense of urgency among movement thinkers making the case that we must not repeat past mistakes and waste this crisis but use it to press for large-scale Green New Deal policies as part of the economic recovery. And yet, strong as this argument is, when the pandemic crisis has passed and the economic rebuilding begins in earnest, we'll still find ourselves under the same political system as before, controlled by the same corporate lobbies, none more powerful than the carbon lobby. And while it may be true that fundamental change never happens without a crisis, it's also the case that the political establishment wants no part of a crisis-level response to climate catastrophe, and that there will be (and already is) overwhelming pressure from establishment Democrats and mainstream liberals to restore "normalcy" and stick with a positive, "unifying" message—one that doesn't "demonize" the industry and its backers, some of whom are Democratic Party funders. But normalcy is precisely what the climate justice movement urgently needs to upend. Normalcy equals catastrophe.

Those who control and profit from the status quo, both

Democrats and Republicans, have worked for years to prevent any true sense of a climate crisis, much less emergency, because they know it means the end of business as usual. That's why it's all the more important that our social movements across a broad progressive front are prepared to create the crisis that the political establishment is desperate to avoid. Otherwise, this "crisis moment," and the opportunity it contains, will disappear—and our best chance at pushing forward with any sort of Green New Deal agenda, to transform the economy as we rebuild it, may very well be lost.

History shows us that nonviolent resistance is more than mere protest, more than merely performative or expressive ("speaking truth to power"); it is essentially strategic. It goes beyond words and symbols. As Gandhi and King and countless others have shown—from the Salt March to the Freedom Rides, from sit-down strikers and draft-card burners to tar-sands blockaders and water protectors—there is no more powerful means of exposing the forces a movement is up against, and no more effective way of forcing an issue, maybe even a reckoning, than sustained and strategic nonviolent direct action.

Is this too much to ask of people emerging from a pandemic and pressed by economic hardship and anxiety? Maybe so. The psychological and material impact of this current crisis is already immense—and our mutual empathy, compassion, and aid is needed. But it's worth reminding ourselves that social movements have often maintained their struggles in the face of extreme adversity—none more so than the radical labor movement of the 1930s (an era increasingly on our minds), when workers fought successfully under harrowing conditions, including brutal violence, few today can imagine; and the Black Freedom Struggle of the 1960s, when people risked and gave their lives for basic civil and human rights. Given the hardship and the incalculable injustice we know the climate catastrophe will bring and is already bringing to the poorest and most marginalized in our society, perhaps the time has come when we need to find a comparable resolve.

Or perhaps there's an analogy with our current situation: Even as scientists race to develop a COVID-19 vaccine and end this pandemic (a positive vision, to say the least), doctors and nurses on the front lines are fighting day and night under extreme conditions to save as many lives as possible, putting themselves at risk. Likewise, even as we push for a Green New Deal, our movement needs more frontline resisters—especially those of us with privilege of various kinds—who are willing and able to throw themselves into the breach, to run toward danger, putting their bodies and freedom on the line. And we need many more people, including corporate and political and cultural leaders, ready and willing to support this resistance. We not only need youth climate strikers filling the streets, we need more and more adults willing to stand in the way—literally—of the carbon-industrial machine.

A recent report from the Yale Program on Climate Change Communication found that 31 percent of Americans would support the use of nonviolent civil disobedience "against corporate or government activities that make global warming worse," and 20 percent would be willing to engage in it themselves. Those are very large, significant numbers. Support for nonviolent resistance in the climate struggle is not marginal or fringe—it's going mainstream. Which is to say, our movement is in fact building the necessary power, if we will use it, to prevent a return to business and politics as usual, end the carbon regime, and prove that another world is possible.

Please stay safe and be well.
Your brother in this struggle

§

On May 25, 2020, George Floyd was murdered in broad daylight by police on the streets of Minneapolis, and the racial-justice uprising of 2020 erupted across the United States and beyond—demonstrating, among many other things, that mass mobilization and resistance was possible, even in a pandemic, if the cause was urgent enough. I and practically every climate activist I know took part in the protests, some devoting themselves full-time.

As of this writing, in mid-2024, there has been no comparable uprising for climate justice—or for democracy.

FOUR

The Hardest Thing

What Global Solidarity Looks Like Now

OCTOBER 2020

Mariana Enriquez grew up on the wrong side of the Riachuelo, the poisoned, lifeless waterway that separates the city of Buenos Aires from the slums to its south. "Four million people without sewers or plumbing," she tells us. The river's proper name, Matanzas—"slaughter"—derives from the slaughterhouses that operated along its banks for two centuries, their animal effluence mixing with industrial and human waste to pollute the water. Among Enriquez's earliest memories is the river's putrid smell, which would wake her up some mornings as a child. And she remembers the floods—only they're worse now, and more frequent, with some neighborhoods flooding twice a month: "The kids go swimming in the streets as if they were pools—the rotten water no longer bothers them."

Sulaiman Addonia is a refugee from Eritrea. As a child he survived war and a Sudanese refugee camp before escaping to London with his older brother, who was then only seventeen. Now he lives in Brussels, where he founded a writing academy for fellow refugees, helping them tell their stories. His partner is a climate activist from a middle-class white family. He used to tell her: "Saving the planet you destroyed is your fight and not mine." But these days

67

he thinks of his family back in Eritrea, one of the world's poorest countries—"the scorching heat they faced, the failed harvests in the region, the decimated workforce," and "the magnificent coral reefs," on which so many lives depend, "dying off"—and he knows the climate is everyone's fight.

Say their names. Mariana Enriquez and Sulaiman Addonia are two of the contributors to *Tales of Two Planets: Stories of Climate Change and Inequality in a Divided World*, a literary anthology edited by John Freeman. I'll admit that this anthology brought back visceral sensations and emotions that I sometimes fear I've grown too numbed to feel anymore. But there they were, my familiar companions: the old grief, the old rage. And, if I'm honest, the old despair that's always lurking. There I am, reading this book on my comfy back porch in an affluent town west of Boston, feeling overwhelmed by my sense of complicity in unspeakable injustices against people, actual human beings, everywhere on Earth—and by my sense of powerlessness as an individual to stop any of it. I could sell my solar-paneled house, live in a yurt, and convert my yard into an organic community garden, and it would make absolutely zero difference to the fates of billions whose names I'll never know and can never say. People with whom I claim to be in solidarity.

If I've learned anything over the past decade covering and engaging in the climate justice movement in this country—the same movement that has pushed the concept of, and varying proposals for, a Green New Deal to the very center of American politics in this election year—it's that "solidarity" is complicated and often elusive. In movement circles, the word and concept of solidarity is all too often used casually, almost thoughtlessly, as if it's a given that all of us fighting for climate justice are in solidarity with each other and with all of those, the vast majority in the Global South, who are on the front lines of climate catastrophe even now. We may believe this, and say it to ourselves and others, but most of the time it simply is not so. Or, at least, not so simple. At the global level, the only level at which humanity's future can and *will* be decided, such solidarity is far from certain.

The idea of global solidarity—any genuine, human solidarity across borders, races, classes, genders, and all the rest—is meaningless without effective action; that is, without action that has some chance of the desired and necessary effect, politically and economically and environmentally. And at the global level—if what one wants is climate justice—such action is eventually going to conflict with national and local priorities and politics. *Even if* the United States, despite the antidemocratic system standing in the way, somehow gets a government reflecting the solid majority who say they want decisive climate action, there will still be the inevitable tension between the local, national, and global.

China is by far the largest source of annual greenhouse emissions on the planet, but the United States, followed by Europe, owes by far the largest "climate debt" to the developing world. This country's historic, cumulative emissions, and continuing per capita emissions, mean that Americans have used and are using far more than their share of the atmospheric "carbon budget" for limiting warming to 1.5 or 2°C. Again, if justice, or simple fairness, is what you care about, this means the United States must move faster and more radically than any other nation on Earth. And while poor and working-class Americans should not be forced to bear the burden, even they are better off, and are responsible for higher per capita emissions, than the global poor—who far outnumber them. (Of course, there are elites throughout the Global South whose per capita emissions rival or exceed those of most Americans.)

This is a hard pill to swallow. And yet the alternative to the

United States paying its global debt is a world without *any* hope of justice, anywhere.

So, yes, the West Coast is burning at a terrifying and unprecedented rate. Yes, Houstonians have suffered *five 500-year floods in five years*, and the Gulf Coast is pummeled by storm after ever more devastating storm, with the poor and racially marginalized suffering most, just as they've long suffered the most from fossil-fuel pollution in their communities. But do any of us really think that Mariana Enriquez's family and neighbors in the Buenos Aires slums have any less right to a healthy, secure life than Americans who lack health care, food security, and clean air and water?

§

At the heart of the case for a Green New Deal, on both the national and global level, is the argument that the choice between justice and human survival is a false one. That is, in order to be politically viable—not to mention ethically defensible—any comprehensive climate strategy to prevent runaway catastrophe must combine rapid decarbonization with economic and social justice because that's the only way to mobilize and sustain a broad coalition to see the job through. That's the idea, anyway.

And if you want to know why the "kids" advocating this vision are perhaps a little angry, and why young people are willing to go to jail to fight for their future, it's because their elders—including intellectuals across the entire political spectrum—have failed them for what is now three decades. They have every right to be pissed off and to demand the kind of political revolution a Green New Deal requires.

Some of that passion comes through in *Winning the Green New Deal: Why We Must, How We Can*, a new collection of essays edited by the Sunrise Movement's Varshini Prakash and Guido Girgenti. With a cast of contributors that includes David Wallace-Wells, Kate Aronoff, Naomi Klein, Bill McKibben, Rhiana Gunn-Wright, Joseph Stiglitz, Julian Brave NoiseCat, the Rev. William J. Barber II, Waleed Shahid, and others, this is the volume that should serve as the definitive introduction to the Green New Deal and the coalition of movements behind it. Even so, it addresses only the United States, not the global context.

Lest we forget, the IPCC makes clear that to have any chance of staying "well below" two degrees of warming, preventing huge swaths of the Global South from becoming uninhabitable—and allowing developing countries some shot at a livable future—*global* greenhouse emissions must fall *by half* in the next ten years and must be all but eliminated by around 2050. The speed and scale of that global shift—truly revolutionary—is almost unimaginable, not for economic reasons (the global economy can afford it) but political reasons, given the unprecedented level of national and international coordination it would require. And as noted, it's a necessity that the United States, Europe, and other Global North economies decarbonize much sooner, if only because they have the technological and economic capability, even as they help mobilize and finance the energy transition in the developing world. This is basic stuff, Climate 101—and it's why the Sunrise-backed Green New Deal calls for a *ten-year* mobilization to decarbonize the US economy as far as technically possible, a far tighter timeline than that of Joe Biden and the Democrats, who aim for 2050. Whether or not a ten-year time frame is actually feasible—and we won't know until we try—the point is that only an all-out effort on that scale by the United States and Europe will offer the hope of meeting the ultimate *global* emissions target for midcentury.

It's one thing to rehearse these numbers and point out that

this is what the world's climate scientists tell us is necessary to salvage a habitable planet. It's another thing entirely to ask poor and working-class Americans, or anyone who has lost a job and faces economic insecurity—in the midst of a pandemic, no less—to take a giant leap of faith that the Green New Deal's promises of jobs, universal health care, racial and environmental justice, and just-transition policies for workers and communities will be fulfilled. Given the polarized and sclerotic political system we've got, why should anyone believe they will? The truth is, nobody knows exactly how a comprehensive Green New Deal will play out, or if it's even possible. And where there are looming unknowns, especially for economically vulnerable people, there will be fear. Most Americans are still more afraid of losing their paycheck than losing the planet. As the French *Gilets Jaunes* (Yellow Vest) movement memorably put it, rebelling against President Emmanuel Macron's ill-conceived and regressive fuel tax: "You talk about the end of the world. We're talking about the end of the month."

And then there is that vast portion of humanity only trying to get through another day.

It's impossible to predict whether the movement for a Green New Deal in the United States, with its emerging coalition of labor unions, racial and environmental justice movements, and a galvanized generation of young people, can spearhead a democratic, bottom-up political revolution to overcome the obstacles of our antidemocratic system. First, there's a make-or-break election to be won—and defended. Beyond that, all we can say with any degree of certainty is that the struggle for a genuine political revolution in this country, to achieve that radical ten-year mobilization, is what global solidarity must look like now.

No such revolution will be possible unless we're willing to level with the public about the dire situation and what those of us in the wealthiest countries owe the rest of the world. Because it will require more of us politically, a higher level of commitment, than anyone in our national politics is yet asking: a willingness to sacrifice, to take risks, to tell the truth no matter how ugly and no matter the consequences. It's going to take all of this on the part of far more people, from all walks of life, than we've ever seen. And if there aren't enough of us willing to take that leap, then we'll soon have to acknowledge that "climate justice" and "global solidarity" are empty phrases—and that Mariana Enriquez's and Sulaiman Addonia's families, and those of countless people like them, are on their own.

Walden at Midnight

Three Walks with the Radical Thoreau

AUGUST 2021

In my walks I would fain return to my senses.
—Henry David Thoreau, "Walking" (1851)

1.

The path to Walden, as you walk north along the western edge of Adams Woods, comes to a fork just beyond the Concord line. If you're heading to Henry Thoreau's most famous pond, you take the trail to the right for a half mile or so, keeping the swampy Andromeda meadows below you on the left, until you cross the tracks of the Fitchburg railroad and you're standing on the shore at Walden's southwest corner looking north across the water toward Henry's cove, his cabin site hidden in the dense woods on the higher ground.

For the past ten years, however, since I discovered this route, I've taken the left fork more often than not, winding down to Fairhaven Bay—the wide expanse of water on the Sudbury River, a hidden lake, really, more or less the size of Walden, with steep, thickly wooded embankments. Many people, even locals, don't know it exists; it's accessible only if you know the trails, or paddle down the river, or happen to own one of the large properties that surround it. Thus it's one of the most secluded and one of the quietest spots in the area, with Walden's crowds a mile away, and still among the best for seeing the local waterfowl.

I've walked this way to Fairhaven several times a year, at least once in each season, since Henry's Journal led me to it a decade ago. But I confess that in more recent years my visits have become rarer. I suppose you could say, as Henry once did, that the remembrance of my country spoiled my walks.

So it felt good on a morning in mid-September of that election year, 2020, to get my head out of my various screens and their endless "takes," and to set out on the trail from Lindentree Farm in Lincoln up through the woods to Fairhaven. The morning was clear and cool, the first maples already showing off their reds, a refreshing early fall day. It was only as I got out of the shadows and into the broad clearings of the farm that I noticed the high atmospheric haze discoloring the sun in an otherwise cloudless sky—smoke carried thousands of miles on the jet stream from the raging, terrorizing wildfires on the other edge of the continent—and realized the sunlight on the ground at my feet and on the stalks and leaves of the crops was slightly dimmed, as though faintly tinted.

Nevertheless, or maybe for that very reason, when I entered the woods at the far side of the farm fields, the details of the forest floor and understory leaped out at me, my senses jolted awake in a way they hadn't been for quite some time. Every leaf and mossed log, every shadow and every sunlit patch of undergrowth became distinct and vivid, as if I'd never seen such a sight before. When I got to Fairhaven I sat on the stone landing by the old boathouse on the north shore. The water was low. Mud stretched several yards in front of me, dotted with lily pads in the muck, and the water's surface was swept by a steady breeze coming straight up the pond from the southwest. A few ducks paddled along, and off to my left, about a hundred yards away, a great blue heron stood statuesque at the water's edge, the subtly altered sunlight glinting on the wavelets.

It struck me that day in September how little the forest and the pond had changed in the ten years since I discovered that spot at Fairhaven. Back then, as I was first really awakening to our planetary crisis, I wondered how much longer we would recognize Henry's woods. But in spite of New England's rising temperatures— our later, warmer autumns, shorter winters, earlier springs—the changes, thus far, have been too subtle for my untrained eyes. But we know far greater change is coming, and soon.

Henry knew these woods around Fairhaven like the proverbial back of his hand. They were his playground, laboratory, sanctuary. "In all my rambles I have seen no landscape which can make me forget Fair Haven," Henry wrote in his Journal at the end of May 1850. "The sight of these budding woods intoxicates me." But they were never a remote or pristine wilderness in his day—indeed they were less so than in ours. They were part and parcel of the surrounding social world. In fact this landscape was far less forested in Henry's time, cleared for farms and grazing land, and the woods were mainly kept for fuel and lumber. Henry saw the landscape change from decade to decade, even year to year. He saw the railroad come through, skirting Walden's west end. And he described, not long after his two-year experiment at the pond, how the woods where he'd lived had been cleared for a farmer's field, and all the evidence that remained of his cabin was the impression of the cellar hole.

Henry was fascinated by the constant cycles of change and regeneration, transience and resilience, whether the timescale was geological or seasonal, or that of human generations. He felt the natural history of the ground he walked. He had deep respect for the Indigenous peoples of Massachusetts and New England, massacred and driven from their lands by Europeans, and he may well have known more about them than any of his contemporaries, researching, conducting interviews, collecting artifacts, as he amassed the several volumes of his pathbreaking "Indian notebooks." For Henry the past and present, human and wild, coexisted in the eternal flux of the here and now.

He had even been the cause of a sudden, violent change in the local landscape. As a young man, in the unusually dry spring of 1844, he and his friend Edward Hoar cooked up a mess of fish on the northeast edge of Fairhaven Bay and accidentally set fire to these very woods. Henry ran to alert the landowners while Edward raised the alarm in Concord, but a hundred acres burned, all the way to the cliffs of Fair Haven Hill, before the townspeople contained it.

Looking back on the experience years later, Henry admitted having felt some guilt, but he quickly got over it, dismissing the complaints of the woods' "owners, so called." He remembered thinking to himself, "I have set fire to the forest, but I have done no wrong therein, and now it is as if the lightning had done it." Indeed, the budding ecologist in him saw the "advantage" of the fire to the local ecosystem, as the Native Americans well knew. "When the lightning burns the forest its Director makes no apology to man, and I was but His agent," he wrote in his Journal. "It is inspiriting to walk amid the fresh green sprouts of grass and shrubbery pushing upward through the charred surface with more vigorous growth."

"That night I watched the fire," he recalled, "where some stumps still flamed at midnight in the midst of the blackened waste."

Henry's scorched earth was the very ground I now walked to Fairhaven.

2.

It wasn't the rosy-fingered dawn rising out of the Aegean, but one early-October morning I saw the sun thrust through the range of clouds on the Atlantic horizon from the high bluff at the Nauset Light, not far from where Henry Thoreau first glimpsed the eastern shore of Cape Cod. Exactly why I was there at that hour, for what purpose, is hard to explain. What compels a man in his fifties to get out of bed three hours before sunrise and drive to the Cape, just so that he can see what a long-dead writer saw and walk where he walked? Though not precisely where he walked—Henry's path along the beach on what is now called the National Seashore has long since gone under the waves.

If you've never viewed it, that eastern edge of Cape Cod from Eastham to Race Point is one wide and all but untouched strip of beach, curving from due north to northwest and west, rimmed by massive sand bluffs that rise at times a hundred feet or more above the waterline, and then become a broad expanse of dunes at the Cape's northern end. For long stretches of the beach, no houses or any other human structures are visible—only sand, bluffs, and ocean as far as the eye can see.

Henry walked the entire thirty-some-odd miles, first with his friend Ellery Channing in October 1849, then again by himself the following summer. I didn't have that kind of time on my hands, so I picked a long, empty section that Henry described in his book *Cape Cod*, north from Newcomb Hollow near the Wellfleet-Truro line.

The temperature that morning was in the low forties, and a battering wind blew out of the north, numbing my cheeks, piercing the fleece I wore. The sky was so clear it was almost dizzying, the ocean a rich, dazzling turquoise and blue, whitecapped to the horizon, the breakers rolling in slantwise to the coast, their salt spray in my face. I walked north for about three miles and back again, alternating from the firmer wet sand to the fine, dry, clean-swept expanse above the tidemark—all in all, more than two hours without seeing another human. The solitude was total; I was utterly alone except for the seabirds and a few curious seals keeping pace with me close to shore, popping their heads out of the water like friendly dogs. But there on the dry sand it was only me. Turning around, I could no longer see where I'd started, my footprints vanishing into the distant glare, and in front of me an infinite vista of sand, sea, and sky. I imagined myself seen from high above, a solitary, melodramatic figure trudging into the hard, relentless wind, as sand blew in sheets across the ground in front of me and over my boots. The bluffs loomed over me, as high and as steep and as rugged as a canyon wall—like some desert landscape in my native Southwest.

We've so domesticated "the beach," nowhere more so than on Cape Cod, that we forget it actually is a kind of desert, just as Henry said. I was walking across a desolate no-man's-land, a death strip for all but the most minutely adapted life-forms—a boneyard for the rest of us.

"They commonly celebrate those beaches only which have a hotel on them," Henry writes in *Cape Cod*. "But I wished to see that seashore where man's works are wrecks." Death is much on his mind in that book, and he tells of how he was once tasked with finding the shark-eaten remains of a human body cast up on the beach a week after a shipwreck. "Close at hand," he writes, these "relics . . . were simply some bones with a little flesh adhering to them. . . . There was nothing at all remarkable about them. . . . But as I stood there they grew more and more imposing. They were alone with the beach and the sea, whose hollow roar seemed addressed to them."

Alone with the beach and sea, I didn't find any bones, human or otherwise, or any evidence of a shipwreck. But I did come across an occasional beached and half-buried lobster trap, broken loose from its mooring. One of them struck me as an art installation, situated on that barren beach as though in some surreal, postapocalyptic gallery. But then I thought about the living human hands that made it and made their living by it. And I thought about the creatures it trapped, and about the warming, acidifying water.

The bluffs have retreated dramatically since Henry's time, thanks to storms and the inexorably rising sea, now a full foot higher. In places, the erosion has exposed the rock and clay midway up the bluffs, as in a canyon wall, and you can see the strata measuring geological time. Elsewhere, a few limbs and roots of trees protrude from the sand on the steep slopes, evidence of the erosion's inland progress.

How far will the water come? If the Greenland and Antarctic ice sheets collapse entirely—and science tells us they eventually will if anything like business as usual continues—then global sea level will ultimately rise more than two hundred feet. The highest of these bluffs will be submerged, as will most of the East Coast. Even in the best-case climate scenarios, requiring revolutionary changes in our politics and economy, we can expect at least a meter of sea-level rise by later this century, possibly within my lifetime. The beach I walked will be a seabed. Henry's beach, somewhere out there where the seals and sharks swim, already is.

"The sea-shore is a sort of neutral ground, a most advantageous point from which to contemplate the world," Henry writes. "Creeping along the endless beach amid the sun-squawl and foam, it occurs to us that we, too, are the product of sea-slime." There on the shore, much as he did on Maine's Mount Katahdin, Henry encountered an inhospitable, inhuman nature:

> It is a wild, rank place, and there is no flattery in it. . . . a
> vast morgue. . . . The carcasses of men and beasts together

lie stately up upon its shelf, rotting and bleaching in the sun and waves. . . . There is naked Nature—inhumanly sincere, wasting no thought on man, nibbling at the cliffy shore where gulls wheel amid the spray.

There at the edge of a continent, the clear horizon revealing the curve of the earth, it occurs to me that I do in fact live on a planet—I, and countless other humans, whose fate means nothing to sand, seawater, or seal. The waves will come, the shore will shift, with or without us, just as it did long before us and always will, long after us.

The so-called Anthropocene matters only to those who conceive of it. To those who suffer it, whether they conceive of it or not, it is only a matter of survival.

3.

In the predawn hours of Sunday morning, December 8, 2019, I stood with a dozen others in the snow on the freight tracks in Ayer, Massachusetts, in front of a train carrying ten thousand tons of West Virginia coal. The train was bound for the power station in Bow, New Hampshire, the last coal-burning plant in New England. That same train had been stopped and blockaded a few hours earlier coming out of Worcester to the south, and it would be blockaded again on the truss bridge across the Merrimack River in Hooksett to the north. Two more coal trains would be blockaded on that route in the weeks ahead. More than a hundred of us (I was among the organizers) were arrested that fall and winter, all part of a sustained grassroots campaign of nonviolent direct action to shut down that coal plant and, ultimately, bring an end to the burning of fossil fuels in New England.

Standing on the tracks in the blinding light of the locomotive, arms linked with my comrades before the sheer mass of the train

and its eighty cars of coal, its immovable weight and iron force—
the smell of the brakes and of coal dust on the frigid air—the over-
powering hum and vibration of the idling diesels rattled my core.

Ten thousand tons of coal, stopped by twelve human bodies—
mothers and fathers, teachers, faith leaders, workers young and
old—for more than an hour. How long could we have stopped it
had there been hundreds of us? Thousands? What would happen if
enough people refused to allow the coal trains to pass?

"Let your life be a counter friction to stop the machine," Henry
Thoreau wrote in the radical abolitionist essay we know as "Civil
Disobedience." If he only knew what the machine would do. I envy
him that he didn't.

We are now in the midst of the sixth mass extinction of species
since life on this planet began—caused this time not by any aster-
oid or natural geological process, but by humanity itself; or, more
specifically, by our global fossil-fuel-driven economic system, those
who make its rules, and those who profit. Scientists estimate that
half of the several million species on Earth will likely face extinction before this century is out.

Of course human life and civilization are also threatened—and
not in some distant dystopian future. In many parts of the world, including parts of this country, catastrophic climate change is already
here. And as always, the poor, the racially marginalized, and the
young—those who have done little or nothing to cause the catastrophe—suffer, and will suffer, most. By 2070, up to one-fifth of the
planet's land area, almost entirely in the poorest parts of the world,
could be rendered uninhabitable by rising heat alone—affecting as
much as one-third of humanity. More than a billion people could be
forced to migrate, becoming climate refugees, by midcentury.

"I walk toward one of our ponds," Henry wrote in "Slavery
in Massachusetts," that furious 1854 address indicting his state's

complicity in the Fugitive Slave Law, "but what signifies the beauty of nature when men are base?"

It was not an idle question.

§

"Walked to Walden last night (moon not quite full) by railroad and upland wood-path, returning by the Wayland road," Henry wrote in his Journal entry for June 13, 1851. Henry was given to walking at night—often following the railroad tracks through the Deep Cut between town and Walden—and he even seemed to prefer it, his senses heightened in the dark. "The woodland paths are never seen to such advantage as in a moonlight night, so embowered, still opening before you almost against expectation as you walk; you are so completely in the woods." And he was especially taken with the sight of the water at night, describing it in almost spiritual terms. "I noticed night before last from Fair Haven how valuable was some water by moonlight . . . reflecting the light with a faint glimmering sheen. . . . The water shines with an inward light like a heaven on earth. The silent depth and serenity and majesty of water! . . . By it the heavens are related to the earth, undistinguishable from a sky beneath you."

Late one night near the end of October, I followed Henry's route, heading south down the tracks from the edge of town, through the Deep Cut, to Walden. The embankments rose steep on either side, the moon hidden somewhere behind the pines towering over me to the west, so that it was very dark as I walked, and I was glad for the flashlight and the walking stick I'd brought. Alone in the suburban woods, in deep autumn silence, I had the pulse-quickened sensation of being in the wild.

And so there I was, purposefully striding down the same

railroad Henry knew, just out for a walk as if nothing out of the ordinary, until I began to think of the history the railroad held, and all it signified. I thought of the Irish laborers fleeing famine who carved that Cut and laid the tracks, and Henry's sympathy and charity toward their families, whose shacks were built into the hillside above the cove on Walden's northwest bank; of the Black fugitives fleeing slavery, whom Henry sheltered and discretely assisted, at no small risk, onto the trains for Canada; of the Harper's Ferry conspirator, a price on his head, whom Henry spirited out of Concord to the station in Acton the day after John Brown was hanged—and of Henry's thundering, radical "A Plea for Captain John Brown."

And I thought of the locomotives, the steam and the coal smoke; the coal itself, the mines, the miners; capital and labor, global industry and technological hubris; empire and oil and Anthropocene.

Half a mile down the tracks, the glow of Walden appeared through the trees, serene and unmeasurable in the distance, and I saw what Henry meant about the water at night. I made my way along the northwest shore—owing to the drought, a narrow strip of gravelly beach rimmed the pond—the only sounds my footsteps and the sudden rustle of startled unseen creatures in the leaves, until I stood on the eastern point of the cove, looking west. I was just in time to see the moon, a waxing gibbous three-fifths full, descending into the tops of the tall pines on the steep opposite shore. There was no reflection on the water, which was entirely calm and still. Its glassy surface caught the faint light of nameless constellations.

A breeze picked up out of the north, sweeping the pond from Henry's cove to the shore below the railroad tracks. My senses were alive and awake as I have rarely felt them, and to my surprise I had no fear of the dark.

"We do not commonly live our life out and full," Henry writes after his night walk to Walden, "we do not fill all our pores with our blood; we do not inspire and expire fully and entirely enough."

"We live but a fraction of our life," he writes there. "Why do we not let on the flood, raise the gates, and set all our wheels in motion? He that hath ears to hear, let him hear. Employ your senses."

What *is* my life, what am I, if not my senses, my body? And what if a life lived out and full requires the readiness to risk it, to give that life entirely, for something or someone beyond my small self, something transcendent yet from which I am not separate— another person, all other persons?

The moon was now hidden. The water at my feet was dark, deep, and clear. It was midnight, and I was alone with Walden.

Wayland, MA
November 2020

PART TWO

Affliction and Revolt

FIVE

The Social Beast

On the Anti-Totalitarianism of Simone Weil

APRIL 2021

It's May 1942 in the city of Marseilles, in what was then Vichy France, and thirty-three-year-old Simone Weil has for the past year been engaged in work for the French Resistance. Though physically frail and racked by migraines, she has among other things helped distribute the underground journal *Cahiers du témoignage chrétien*, launched by three clergymen in early 1941, delivering three hundred copies of each of its first three issues. The personal risk is considerable. As Robert Zaretsky tells us in *The Subversive Simone Weil* (2021), one of her fellow couriers was arrested and deported, and Weil herself was twice hauled in and interrogated by the police. But the calm, formidable philosopher, activist, and talker was released both times. When she was sent home, Zaretsky notes, "the sense of relief at the station must have been palpable."

Now, as she reluctantly prepares to leave for the United States with her parents (for their safety, not her own), Weil writes a series of long letters to an antifascist, philosemitic Catholic priest named Joseph-Marie Perrin. The young Father Perrin, about the same age as Weil, has become her friend and de facto confessor, though she has not accepted baptism into the Church—and never will—and thus, according to Catholic dogma, cannot receive the sacraments. In her intensely intellectual, profoundly personal letters to Perrin, published posthumously in *Waiting for God* (1951), Weil relates her rather unusual "spiritual autobiography." Raised, as Zaretsky puts it, in a "fiercely nonobservant" haute-bourgeois Jewish family in Paris, having never entered a synagogue, Weil was attracted early to Catholicism, its liturgy, music, and art. But it was only in her late twenties—first while visiting an impoverished fishing village in Portugal, then a Romanesque church in Assisi, and finally, climactically, the Abbey of Solesmes in northern France, famed for its monks' Gregorian chant—that she experienced a spiritual, what many have called mystical, awakening to Christian faith.

Most important, though, in these letters she wants to explain to Perrin why she has chosen to refuse baptism and remain outside the Catholic Church, whatever the consequences for her soul. Pointing to "an absolutely insurmountable obstacle" that stands in her way, Weil writes to Perrin, "It is the use of the two little words *anathema sit.* . . . I remain beside all those things that cannot enter the Church . . . on account of those two little words. I remain beside them all the more because my own intelligence is numbered among them." For Weil, what that Latin phrase represents—the sentence of excommunication, banishment, and even, historically, torture and death imposed upon those deemed heretics—carried more than religious significance. A few pages later, she writes, "After the fall of the Roman Empire, which had been totalitarian, it was the Church that was the first to establish a rough sort of totalitarianism in Europe. . . . This tree bore much fruit. And the motive power of this totalitarianism was the use of those two little words: *anathema sit.*" It was by that same kind of power, transposed into secular use, Weil tells the priest, "that all the parties which in our own day have founded totalitarian regimes were shaped."

Weil had little more than a year to live when she handed down that judgment—she died in August 1943 of tuberculosis and her own refusal to eat, in a sanatorium outside London, where she had gone to work with de Gaulle's Free French. And while she's remembered as much today for her secular political and moral philosophy—not to mention the sheer force of her indomitable personality—as she is for her deeply, weirdly Christian theological writings, the letters to Father Perrin seem to hold a key to her life and thought. And what she meant by that word *totalitarian*—whether referring to the Roman Catholic Church, Nazism and Stalinism, or the tendencies of political parties and organizations in general (she wrote a pamphlet titled "On the Abolition of All Political Parties")—hangs over it all. Like others in her own time and since, Weil not only used *totalitarian* in a literal sense, to refer to specific all-powerful and controlling state systems. She also used it in a more figurative or cultural sense, as a repressive mindset, a coercive social and institutional tendency, an intrinsic characteristic of the all-devouring "collective passions," what she sometimes called the "social Beast."

Weil's use of this charged term, in particular what she called the "totalitarian spirituality" of the medieval Church, feels uniquely relevant to our own moment, with our contemporary plagues of white "Christian" nationalism, colonialism (which Weil spoke against in her own day), Big Tech hegemony, and even, ultimately, our planetary ecological catastrophe. It has to do with how Weil saw both theology and ideology, combined with power, as dehumanizing forces—in the way they treat human beings as abstractions (something our social media takes to a whole new level), and then turn them into mere things, cogs in the machinery, mindless slaves, and finally, corpses. Revisiting her story reminds us that not only Weil's ideas but her life as well offer a bracing, often unsettling challenge to any of us who would resist our own totalitarian tendencies, individual and collective, today.

§

It's hard if not impossible to imagine a figure of Weil's stature in the intellectual and political culture of today's left, the only region of the political spectrum where she might possibly fit. And not just because of her religiosity, which would instantly ghettoize her in many left spaces (though by no means all). It's also because she's so hard to pin down with any neat, easy label—or rather, because the labels are too many and apparently conflicting. (She'd be eaten alive on Twitter from all sides—or, worse, simply shunned and ignored.) "An anarchist who espoused conservative ideals," Zaretsky writes in his opening pages, "a pacifist who fought in the Spanish Civil War, a saint who refused baptism, a mystic who was a labor militant, a French Jew who was buried in the Catholic section of an English cemetery, a teacher who dismissed the importance of solving a problem, the most willful of individuals who advocated the extinction of the self: here are but a few of the paradoxes Weil embodied."

The key word there is *embodied*. As Zaretsky succinctly puts it, "Simone Weil fully *inhabited* her philosophy." To understand Weil one has to see her whole, in three dimensions, as a full and fully engaged human being, even if she at times comes off as incoherent—a lot like life itself. Then again, a little incoherence may not be such a bad thing, especially when the alternative is the enforced false coherence of a totalizing theological or ideological system.

Much as he did for Camus in 2013's *A Life Worth Living: Albert Camus and the Quest for Meaning*, Zaretsky lucidly guides us through Weil's complexities. Because as much as there is to admire about Weil, she can be confoundingly difficult and, as Zaretsky admits, irritating, even insufferable, in her uncompromising judgments. No one, herself included, could live up to her standards. She was a philosopher and mystic who revolted against any merely abstract ideology or theology. For Weil, it was always about the actual person, the actual experience, the immediate world, whether a classroom, a factory, or a farm; a battlefield or a church. Philosophy, ethics, and religion had to be *lived* in order to be worth anything—and she tried to put this exacting ethos into practice, which often led her to extremes (she rationed her own meals in solidarity with the malnourished). When it came to resistance, for Weil, mouthing slogans was never enough—it required rigorous thought, moral clarity, and action. Fitting, then, that it was Camus who championed and published her posthumously when he was at Gallimard in Paris following the war. When he was asked upon receiving the Nobel, in 1957, to name the writers to whom he felt closest personally, Weil was one of only two (the other was René Char). Though he'd never met her in life, he considered her a friend.

And it was from Weil's own experience that her most distinctive and perhaps most important concept—*malheur* (affliction)—emerged, without which we can't grasp what she meant by *totalitarian* in the fullest sense. In the early 1930s, after graduating from the elite École Normale Supérieure—where she was flamboyantly absorbed in revolutionary politics, with strong anarcho-syndicalist sympathies (she never joined the Communist Party)—Weil taught philosophy to lycée students in provincial towns and tirelessly kept up her engagement in the labor movement, teaching night classes for workers in small industrial cities. And as she deepened her contact with the workers, she began to lose faith in revolution. While she admired Marx's analysis of capitalism, she found the Marxist theory of history a sort of fable, or as Zaretsky aptly puts it, an abstract "millenarian eschatology," detached from the realities of working-class life.

By late 1934, coming to see that an effective working-class politics would need to be rooted in the actual experience of working-class people, she took a fateful and characteristically drastic step: she got a job on the floor of the Alsthom electronic equipment factory in Paris, working long hours operating a stamping press and other heavy machinery under brutal and demeaning conditions. Always physically awkward and weak, eating little and prone to searing headaches, Weil pushed herself to exhaustion and despair alongside her fellow women workers. Inevitably, the job didn't last (whether she was fired or just physically worn out is unclear), yet she managed to get work in two more factories over the course of a year, seriously compromising her health. She emerged a changed person and thinker. She believed that she had gained insight into the dehumanized condition of a slave, and she called this condition *malheur*.

There's no word in English that truly captures the meaning of Weil's *malheur*, but translators have settled on "affliction." In a lengthy essay she left with Father Perrin, Weil offers her best description. "In the realm of suffering," she writes, "affliction is something apart, specific, and irreducible. . . . It takes possession of the soul and marks it through and through with its own particular mark, the mark of slavery." While affliction always involves pain or the fear of pain (including mental or emotional), she goes on to clarify, "There is not real affliction unless the event that has seized and uprooted a life attacks it, directly or indirectly, in all its parts, social, psychological, and physical. The social factor is essential. There is not really affliction unless there is social degradation or the fear of it in some form or another."

By the time she wrote that essay, with the Nazi Wehrmacht bearing down, Weil believed "affliction is hanging over us all." And affliction for Weil in the deepest sense, unsurprisingly given her mystic turn, is somehow more than the sum of its identifiable parts: its effect is also inescapably spiritual. Affliction, she writes, "deprives its victims of their personality and makes them into things. It is indifferent; and it is the coldness of this indifference—a metallic coldness—that freezes all those it touches right to the depths of their souls. . . . They will never believe any more that they are anyone." When Christ on the cross cried out to God, "Father, why have you forsaken me?," he was afflicted, Weil tells us. "Extreme affliction . . . is a nail whose point is applied at the very center of the soul. . . . [Affliction] introduces into the soul of a finite creature the immensity of force, blind, brutal, and cold. . . . He struggles like a butterfly pinned alive into an album." Love itself, which for Weil means love of God and neighbor, is the only thing that can still reach the afflicted, if they can only hold on to it themselves. "Through all the horror," she writes, the afflicted "can continue to want to love."

Affliction is the consequence of all-consuming, soul-crushing external force. It is what dehumanizing power—physical, psychological, spiritual—does to a person, whether that power is wielded by a church, a state, a corporation, a political party or movement, or an entire political and economic system. The force that afflicts—that which enslaves, literally or figuratively—is totalitarian.

§

It seems safe to suggest that there are many today who would recognize what Weil was talking about, or who at least have some inkling of how it feels. Indeed, it's frightening how closely her concept of affliction fits what our technocapitalist, social media saturated existence is doing to us politically and culturally. When a person is reduced, by outside forces beyond their control, to an abstract category—a race, a gender, a sexual orientation, a class, a religion, a nationality, a political label, a demographic—they begin to feel the cold vise of affliction. Whatever our various identities, wherever we may fall on the ideological spectrum, we're in the grip of a dehumanizing force.

When American churches—both Catholic and evangelical Protestant—or any other religious institutions preach a form of religion, so-called "Christian" or otherwise, that defines human beings in abstract theological terms as worthy and unworthy, included and excluded, they effectively employ those two little words, *anathema sit*. And when those same churches and religious institutions align with a political party that defines itself in terms of racial and religious nationalism, affliction is the result—whether it looks like caged migrant children; or incarcerated, pandemic-stricken bodies; or members of Congress hunted by neofascists in the hallways of the Capitol.

When a political and economic system degrades and dehumanizes workers, the unemployed, and the unhoused of whatever race or gender or religion, there is affliction. When large segments of a society are abandoned to "deaths of despair," there is affliction.

When technology companies design all-pervasive social media platforms to prey algorithmically upon human weakness, neurological and emotional and moral—and to profit from the exponential amplification of institutionalized mendacity through ever-multiplying echo chambers of mindless collective abuse of the abstract Other, so that *no one*, of any identity or ideology, is spared the coercive pressure of conformity and fear of punishment—something very like affliction becomes the general condition of a society.

It even begins to look as though affliction is now a planetary condition. When the prevailing technocratic carbon-industrial regime that runs the global economy pursues a nihilistic course of limitless fossil-fueled growth, or a greenwashed version of the same, so that entire populations of human beings—first and foremost across the Global South—are rendered superfluous (Hannah Arendt's term) for the sake of profit and power, then we see that the climate catastrophe itself is driven by a kind of totalitarian force. Weil, who was fiercely anticolonialist, argued in her final work, *The Need for Roots*, that the uprooting of peoples, the destruction of cultures and traditions and entire histories—as the colonizing powers of white Christendom had been doing for centuries—counted as crimes of the largest magnitude. Historical and cultural rootedness, Weil firmly believed, is a fundamental human need. In our time, fossil-fueled capital turns Indigenous homelands into wastelands or drowns them under the waves.

It was those uprooted and afflicted global masses, both far and near, with whom Weil stood in solidarity to the end of her short, subversive, and tragic life—a life, as Zaretsky suggests, that was a fully embodied act of resistance. Weil's whole purpose, philosophically and morally, was to *know* her fellow human beings *as human beings*, not abstractions—to understand what they experienced and suffered by living and working alongside them in farm fields, factories, and fishing boats; devoting her time to tutoring those she came in contact with, opening their minds; risking her life alongside them in Spain and with the French Resistance. In both the literal and the broadest sense, she lived an anti-totalitarian life.

§

But we can't leave it there, tempting as it may be. That's because Weil's most unsettling contradiction was her attitude toward her own Jewish heritage, as seen in several of her comments on Israel and Judaism that are widely read as antisemitic. Zaretsky, who

is Jewish and has written movingly of his own struggle to speak
about the Holocaust, squarely confronts this disturbing aspect of
Weil's thought. What's clear is that Weil saw the ancient Hebrew
religion as a form of oppressive and at times genocidal religious
nationalism, based on the core dogma of Israel as "chosen people"—a concept Weil abhorred in any context. ("There is no such
thing as a holy nation," she writes in *The Need for Roots*.) She considered both ancient Israel *and* her other great enemy, the Roman
Empire, as precursors to twentieth-century totalitarianism. But it
also seems clear—given Weil's staunch opposition to Nazism and
its oppression of Jews—that her horror was directed at the theology
and national ideology of ancient Israel, not at Jews as people, which
would obviously negate everything she wrote about the sanctity
of each human being. Zaretsky tells us that Father Perrin tried
to convince her that she was mistaken in her readings of Hebrew
scripture, but whatever the case, there's little doubt she was deeply
alienated from Judaism.

All of which leaves a bad taste—and can't help but color Weil's
attraction to Christianity. And yet this is also why her inner struggle with Roman Catholic dogma and the Church as an institu-
tion is crucial. Because as we know, it wasn't just Israel and ancient
Rome that she saw as totalitarian precursors; it was every bit as
much the medieval Church, with its persecution and extermina-
tion of heretics and infidels. "What frightens me is the Church as
a social structure," she wrote to Perrin. "I am afraid of the Church
patriotism existing in Catholic circles. . . . I am afraid of it because
I fear to catch it. . . . There were some saints who approved of the
Crusades or the Inquisition . . . they were blinded by something
very powerful."

Zaretsky notes that Weil's theological turn in her later years
"marked a rupture" for many readers. "But for others," he writes,

"it is less a break than a broadening of the same concerns that had always driven her thought." So it's surprising that Zaretsky makes little of Weil's decision to remain outside the Church—even though, for a Christian believer, no decision could be weightier. Alan Jacobs, in a moving portrait of Weil in *The Year of Our Lord 1943: Christian Humanism in an Age of Crisis* (2018), sees greater significance in Weil's refusal of baptism, framing it as central to her life and moral commitments. Indeed, it was perhaps her ultimate and most profound act of human solidarity—and perhaps her most subversive. In one of her letters to Father Perrin before leaving Marseilles with her parents, Weil makes the astoundingly bold confession: "It seems to me that the will of God is that I should not enter the Church at present." In fact, she tells the priest, when she thinks of baptism and entering the Church, "nothing gives me more pain than the idea of separating myself from the immense and unfortunate multitude of unbelievers."

"I have the essential need, and I think I can say the vocation," Weil continues, in what could be a summation of her faith and philosophy, "to move among men of every class and complexion, mixing with them and sharing their life and outlook, so far that is to say as conscience allows, merging into the crowd and disappearing among them, so that they show themselves as they are, putting off all disguises with me. It is because I long to know them so as to love them just as they are. For if I do not love them as they are, it will not be they whom I love, and my love will be unreal."

SIX

Great Sinners

Dostoevsky, My Father, and Me

MARCH 2022

In four years in prison I came at last to distinguish men among criminals.
—Fyodor M. Dostoevsky, letter to his brother Mikhail, February 22, 1854

1. Sin and Suffering

In the dream I'm standing with Dostoevsky on the scaffold, as though I'm seeing through his eyes as he and his comrades, convicted of political crimes, await execution. It's December 22, 1849, and in the scene that unfolds on the ground below in St. Petersburg's Semenovsky Square, the first three of the condemned men are tied to stakes before a firing squad. Fyodor Mikhailovich appears to be in the next group, and he's certain that he has only a few minutes left to live. On the scaffold (as Joseph Frank describes it in his monumental biography), Dostoevsky turns to Nikolay Speshnev—who twenty years later would be an inspiration for the nihilist Stavrogin in *Demons*—and says, "We shall be with Christ." To which Speshnev replies, smiling strangely, "A bit of dust."

Of course, the firing squad never fired. The mock execution was staged, to the last detail, according to the tsar's personal instructions. A messenger galloped dramatically into the square to announce that Nicholas I, in his great mercy, had commuted their sentences to Siberian prison and exile. Dostoevsky got four years at hard labor, followed by four more in the ranks at an isolated garrison on the southern steppe—all for the crime of conspiring to print and distribute subversive writings.

One of Dostoevsky's comrades, his nerves already broken by the eight months of solitary confinement they had endured, was shattered by the mock execution. But Dostoevsky, though deeply shaken, was nothing short of reborn. That is, reborn but not yet transformed. That would require the next four years in the *katorga*, the vast system of Siberian forced-labor camps, years he semi-fictionalized in the autobiographical novel *Notes from a Dead House*, published in 1861, only two years after his return from exile. There in the harsh military prison camp within the fortress at Omsk, he experienced what many would later call one of the great moral-spiritual awakenings in world literature, and Fyodor Mikhailovich, you might say, became Dostoevsky.

Early on in *Notes from a Dead House*, he offers a glimpse of how this process began. As an educated nobleman (even if from the lower ranks), Dostoevsky's narrator is cut off from all but a handful of his fellow convicts by a chasm of social class and privilege, and he soon realizes that he knows nothing of these men and how they think and feel. He'll have to reexamine, if not throw out entirely, his utopian socialist assumptions and any kind of simplistic idealization of the poor and downtrodden. Indeed, he meets with extremes of moral depravity, along with depths of desperation and hopelessness, previously unimagined. One prisoner, the narrator tells us (in Richard Pevear and Larissa Volokhonsky's translation), was said to have "put a knife into a man just like that, for nothing, for an onion." Another, we're told, "cuts little children's throats for the pleasure of it, to feel their warm blood on his hands, to enjoy their fear, their last dove-like trembling under his knife." Others, he comes to understand, have committed their crimes precisely "so as to get to hard labor and thus rid themselves of an even harder life in freedom." Still another tells the story of how he savagely beat and murdered his wife for confessing she loved another man, to which his listener replies coolly: "Hm. . . . Of course, if you don't beat them—no good'll come of it!" (The latter chapter-length scene is just one of Dostoevsky's numerous cries on behalf of oppressed women.)

Perhaps most troubling, he finds it impossible to read the souls of his fellow prisoners. "I did not see the least sign of repentance among these people, nor the least heavy brooding on their crime," his narrator tells us near the outset. "On the other hand, who can say he has probed the depths of these lost hearts and read in them what is hidden from the whole world? . . . No, crime, it seems, cannot be comprehended from given, ready-made points of view."

In fact, the complexity and moral chaos of the humanity he now encounters in prison would seem to defy the rational modes of explanation he has learned to rely on, and this leads Dostoevsky to a philosophical reflection that seems to point toward a new trajectory in his thought and writing. Trying to divide the convicts among the "good," the "wicked," and "those in total despair," the narrator steps back and admits: "However, here I am now trying to sort our whole prison into categories; but is that possible? Reality is infinitely diverse compared to all, even the most clever, conclusions of abstract thought." Acutely sensitive to the hostility of the peasant convicts toward educated gentlemen like himself, he yearns for some tangible human connection to break through the barriers of class, yet without deluding himself that they can be erased. "We're all people, all human beings. But the idea is too abstract."

"In prison it sometimes happened that you would know a man for several years and think he was a beast, not a man, and despise him," the narrator goes on. "And suddenly a chance moment would come when his soul, on an involuntary impulse, would open up and you would see in it such riches, feeling, heart, such a clear understanding of his own and others' suffering, as if your own eyes had been opened . . ."

But nothing touches a deeper chord in Dostoevsky than the Russian Orthodox rituals in preparation for Holy Week, leading up to Easter, when the prisoners were "taken under armed convoy to the house of God." Huddled with his fellow convicts just inside the doors, he recalls standing in church as a child and seeing "the simple folk thickly crowding by the entrance," and thinking, "they were not praying as we were, they were praying humbly, zealously, bowing to the ground." Now he finds himself in the same position, only "shackled and disgraced," and paints a scene that could be straight from the Old Masters. "The prisoners prayed very assiduously," he tells us, "and each of them each time brought his beggarly kopeck to church for a candle or the collection. 'I'm also a human being,' he may have thought or felt as he gave it. 'Before God we're all equal.'" During the communion liturgy, the narrator continues, "when the priest holding the chalice recited the words '... but like the thief accept me,' almost everybody fell to the ground, their fetters clanking."

These occasional flashes of light alleviate the otherwise relentlessly bleak and brutal description of convict life—the cold, the cramped barracks, the food, the fear, the inhuman floggings, the stench and death of the hospital ward. And yet Dostoevsky refused to sentimentalize or idealize the "human spirit" of his fellow prisoners. He won't let the reader forget that most of these men are capable of terrible things. They are both criminals *and* men, complex individuals, sinners and sufferers.

Some would no doubt prefer Dostoevsky without all the religion—they want the psychological, murder-obsessed, secular-philosophical Dostoevsky—but that's like trying to have Marx without his theory of history. Dostoevsky's deep-rooted religious faith—with all its intense internal struggle and its confounding, disturbing contradictions—is central. At its best, it was a kind of all-embracing Christian humanism; at its worst, in his last years, it served a combative Russian Orthodox nationalism.

In 1869, as he was finishing *The Idiot*—his less-than-satisfying attempt to bring an entirely good man to life, Christlike but fallibly human—Dostoevsky started outlining a huge new multivolume novel, or series of novels, which he would call *The Life of a Great Sinner*. Never written, various elements of it show up in *Demons* and *The Brothers Karamazov*. In Dostoevsky's notes, the protagonist, his "great sinner," undergoes a life-altering crisis of faith, wanders Russia and Europe in search of "an idea," and spends time in a monastery under the direction of the Russian saint Tikhon. "He finally comes to rest in Christ," Dostoevsky projected, "but his whole life is storm and disorder." The historical Tikhon of Zadonsk was said to have himself experienced a "dark night of the soul," and at the heart of the planned novel would be the principle, in Tikhon's own words, "There is no kind of sin, and there cannot be any such on earth, that God would not pardon to someone who sincerely repents."

Today, it's true, the word *sin* has an almost archaic sound to it. But perhaps it has its uses, even for the most militantly religion-free. The question still presents itself: What are we to do about the "great sinners" among us? Not the most extreme cases, the psychopathic mass murderers, totalitarian torturers, the incorrigibly evil, who can only be removed from society. I mean the far greater number who, despite their "redeeming qualities," their "better angels"—their capacity for humane feeling, compassion, love—nevertheless willfully cause great harm and suffering. They may have suffered greatly themselves, and yet for reasons they most likely do not understand—because we're talking about something deeper, often subrational—these otherwise ordinary souls (if we're honest, ourselves included?) turn their suffering outward and inflict it upon others, including the innocent and defenseless, whether strangers or those closest to them. And how do we relate to them, live alongside of them, when we ourselves love them—or want to love them—and when those we love, even we ourselves, are the victims?

These are eternal questions, and there will never be any final answers or ready-made formulas. But let us acknowledge, at the very least, that these questions are real and pressing—never more so, perhaps, than at a moment in history when people in this country and everywhere must decide whether they can live with one another as citizens, neighbors, fellow members of a human family.

2. Confession

When I started dreaming of Dostoevsky, I knew it had become an obsession. So, tell me, what else was there to do, in the midst of a plague, except yield to it? For two years, I'd been reading and re-reading all of his major novels and was now deep into the Frank biography. There was no turning back—the only way out was through.

I should also probably explain, before I go any further, that I lost both of my parents in the plague. They didn't die *of* the plague, that is, of COVID-19, but they died during it—and at their age, approaching ninety, in steep physical and cognitive decline, under quarantine, in the time before vaccines brought some relief, it was in some ways almost the same. The plague—the isolation and lone-liness, the enforced confinements, desolate absences—defined their end. They were its prisoners.

Not that there's anything remarkable about this, or about the one writing it. I'm just a white, straight, cis, married, middle-aged American male with two young-adult children and a house in an affluent town west of Boston where I've lived for twenty-five years. Of course, like so many others, I'm not from around here. I was born and raised in southern California, near LA, with roots in rural, working-class, small-town Texas, and with the fraught in-heritance of a conservative, evangelical, Bible Belt upbringing. But there's nothing very remarkable about any of that either. I'm not going to tell you my life story—only certain facts that seem relevant to the topic at hand.

To begin with, there's the fact that my parents were deeply in love, that they met and married in their late teens; he came from sharecroppers, her father was a rural mail carrier. There's also the fact that they were, both of them, emotionally volatile, even un-stable, given to explosive outbursts of uncontrolled anger and long, draining, fearsome fights. These scenes were countless and frayed the nerves of their children—myself and my three older sisters. Our parents separated several times, yet with the counseling of pastors, church elders, and friends, they would somehow be "reconciled."

It is also a fact that they were both, and especially my mother, devout, gentle and affectionate, generous and sentimental, and not least of all funny. My mother loved to laugh, and to laugh with oth-ers, as if laughter, like prayer, like breath, were necessary to live, the antidote to suffering. Most of the laughter, and most of the prayer, of course, was hers—as was most of the suffering.

I want to be clear: my father was not a bad man. His better an-gels were, in the end, better than most. But he did some bad things, some of them very bad, which cannot be forgotten.

I'll try to say this as simply and straightforwardly as possible. One morning at the breakfast table when I was in fourth grade (the only child left in the house, my sisters having graduated from high school), I witnessed my father commit what can only be called a violent crime, a vicious and brutal act. The victim was my mother. The memory has never left me, remains uncannily clear, and still comes, unbidden, without warning. It lives inside me, in my body.

I don't remember how it started. I only know that they were arguing more intensely than usual, and there was something desperate in my mother's voice, and my stomach seized up in that too-familiar way so that I lost my appetite. And then this happened: My father took a small piece of paper that she had handed him, with something written on it, and wadded it up into a ball, and he told my mother that she was going to eat it, or he'd make her. And then he was on his feet, and he was holding her down in her seat across the table from me, and she was crying out, and then her cry became muffled, garbled, a groaning, and he was trying to shove the wad of paper into her mouth, and she was struggling, and he was yelling something, I don't know what, something unintelligible to me, and one hand gripped her jaw and the other crammed the balled-up paper into her mouth, which was now bleeding profusely as she struggled. It happened fast, and also very slowly, or maybe that's only in my mind, but I remember that I was on my feet, and I was yelling something in my small, pathetic voice, like "Daddy stop! Daddy stop!" and he didn't stop, as though he didn't hear me, didn't even notice me. And then it was over. He walked out of the room, without apology, and I saw the damp and bloody wad of paper on the table. I'll never know what it said, but I know that my mother's lower front teeth had pierced all the way through the skin between her lip and her chin, and blood was pouring out, and she was sobbing and calling after him—crying out that she, she herself, was sorry—and her cries were like nothing human I had ever heard. And then I remember that he was gone, and I was standing at the front door as she sent me off to school—which was just up the street and around the corner, so that I usually walked— and she hugged me and assured me, as she held a wet washcloth with ice against her mouth, that she would be okay, and that she loved me, and that everything would be okay.

I'd seen him get physical with her before, of course. I'd seen him shove her down onto their bed. I'd seen him threaten her in an argument, leaning over her and jabbing his finger in her face. One of my sisters, when they lived in Texas before I was born, once heard her screaming and ran into their room to find her backed up against the wall, his hands around her throat. But I had never witnessed anything like the sheer brutality and violence of that morning. In that moment, I've since understood, my world shattered. Whatever moral authority my father still possessed, after all I'd seen and heard, was destroyed and swept away. He had reduced my mother to a writhing mass of flesh—teeth and lips and blood— right in front of my young eyes, and had walked away without a word to me, as if I didn't exist. If such an act could go unpunished and our lives could go on as before—if he could go on being my father and I his son, bound by the will of God to respect and obey him, as the Bible said I must—then there could be no moral order in my nine-year-old universe.

For whatever reason—shame? remorse? fear of consequences?— nothing like that scene ever happened again, and he never spoke to me of it. But from that day on, every argument, every raised voice I heard through my bedroom walls, sent a surge of fear through my young limbs. I can still feel it.

It's not that I have no good memories of him, but they're from before, when I was much younger. My mother would let me stay up late until he got home from the office, and after he ate dinner he'd lie down on the couch, and I'd stretch out on his broad barrel of a chest and fall asleep to the rise and fall of his breathing and the sound of his voice as he rubbed my back and told me stories of his own childhood, with his older brothers and sisters on the farm in Texas in the 1930s and '40s, until those memories, the best ones, the ones he'd clung to, became mine. But the older I got, and the more I saw and understood, the more I learned only to fear him—and the fear strangled the affection, and the fear became rage.

I confess that, for a time in my early twenties, I wanted to kill him.

The summer before my senior year in college, he left my mother for another woman. That's when I started dreaming of killing my father with my bare hands—I was strong and athletic, he was middle-aged and out of shape, and the most terrifying thing was that I knew I could take him, and I saw myself doing it. Of course, it never went beyond the dream—I remained the obedient son and went along with the new arrangements, was polite to his new wife, God help her.

My parents' divorce dragged on for years—they owned their own small business, and my mother had helped build it. Before it was all settled, my mother experienced a mental breakdown, was admitted to a psychiatric hospital, and was treated for severe depression and anxiety with, as the doctor put it, "psychotic features." She recovered, with the help of medication and therapy and the love of her friends and her children—and, more than anything, her faith.

Maybe the most impressive thing about my mother, perhaps the great achievement of her life, was that her Christian faith—though not without her own dark nights of the soul—was rooted in hope and love, not the fear and judgment characteristic of her strict fundamentalist upbringing in West Texas. Her favorite Psalm was the forty-sixth, as the renowned Hebrew scholar Robert Alter translates it: "God is a shelter and strength for us. . . . 'Let go, and know that I am God.'" The Jesus of the Gospels, the Jesus of compassion, of all-embracing and unconditional love, was real to her, present in her prayers. By some miracle she escaped, for the most part, the bigotries of her environment. (My father, alas, was less successful.) She loved her neighbor, whomever they might be, with an active, not abstract, love. She was "poor in spirit," humble, acutely aware of her own sins, such as they were, and begged forgiveness of God and of all of us. She taught us forgiveness. "When someone is the most unlovable," she would say, "is precisely when they need love the most." She knew this because, sometimes, it meant her.

After eight years in what one might call a wilderness, my father left his second wife, and came back to my mother, all but crawling on his knees, and asked, I believe sincerely, for her forgiveness—and his children's. And, yes, after everything he'd done, she took him back. You couldn't write a better parable—the Prodigal Husband. And so she married him a second time, and they lived the rest of their days together, and we became, almost, a happy family.

She died on the afternoon of Saturday, June 6, 2020, in a hospital south of Nashville, where they lived in their last years near my eldest sister and her daughter. At eighty-nine, her dementia was advancing, and she'd suffered a bad fall in their small apartment at the assisted-living home, fractured her pelvis, and developed internal bleeding. For two months during that spring of 2020, she was moved back and forth from hospital rooms to rehabilitation facilities, under constant quarantine, no visitors allowed. My father—alone, all but blind, practically deaf, quarantined in that small apartment, Fox News blaring—never saw her again.

When it became clear that she wouldn't recover, and we were told that family could visit her, I threw my things in the car and drove the eighteen hours from Boston to Nashville, praying I'd make it in time. When I got there, to my amazement, she was awake in her room, talkative, in good spirits. It was her last afternoon as herself. We even had a few laughs.

By the next morning she was asleep and slipping into an ever-deeper unconsciousness. Her breathing, though, was peaceful, unlabored, and unassisted. I had downloaded the Bible on my tablet, and hoping she could hear me, I read aloud to her from her favorite scriptures, all the most comforting passages she'd read to me as I fell asleep in my bed as a child. And I sang old favorite hymns, the ones she always remembered her father singing. She was close to her father, and like him, she had a beautiful voice.

That Friday night, at around 9 p.m., my father found the courage to call, and I put my phone near her ear. There we were again, the three of us, and I listened in the darkened room as my father struggled to say goodbye to the woman who had loved him, actually loved him, like no other person ever would, or could.

Late that night I went back to my hotel room to try to sleep a little, and I woke at 3 a.m. crying. I was back at the hospital early, and when I saw her, I knew. Her breathing was barely audible, her face drawn, sunken, pale, yet without any sign of pain. My sister and I sat with her, talking so she'd hear our voices, until out of nowhere she took a deep, elongated breath, and then another, and another, at lengthening intervals, but without struggle, without gasps—and we stood by the bed, said soothing words, gently held her hands. I stroked her forehead and the hair brushed back at her temple, and sang to her, and she was gone.

It was a "good death," as they say, as if the Good Lord decided that this good and faithful servant had suffered enough for one lifetime, so why make her suffer any more in leaving it.

Yes, if there is a good Lord who decides such things, that must surely be what He would decide.

3. Judgment

"I need retribution, otherwise I will destroy myself. And retribution not somewhere in infinity, but here and now, on earth," Ivan Karamazov tells his younger brother, Alyosha, as they sit in the local tavern in the pivotal "Rebellion" chapter of *The Brothers Karamazov* (again in the Pevear and Volokhonsky translation).

Ivan is the "great sinner" of *Brothers K.*, though he has some stiff competition, not least his debauched and lecherous father, Fyodor Pavlovich, and his profligate and violent brother Dmitri. Only Ivan, however (as Dostoevsky's image of the radical intellectuals of the day), goes all the way and rebels against God, plunging headlong into the moral abyss in which, according to reason, "everything is permitted." It is Ivan, possessed by his "idea," who gives "permission" to his father's murderer—and Ivan's belated realization of his own culpability provides the coup de grâce to his teetering sanity. But there in the tavern, face-to-face with Alyosha—still a novice monk under the direction of the saintly Elder Zosima (Dostoevsky's tribute to Tikhon)—Ivan reveals the inner torment at the source of his rebellion: the problem of theodicy and the suffering of innocents, especially children.

Ivan is a great cataloger of atrocities, as was Dostoevsky, and he has just told Alyosha of a wealthy landowner who sicced his dogs on an eight-year-old serf boy, who was torn apart as his mother watched, because the boy had thrown a rock at one of the hounds; and of a five-year-old girl, abused by her parents, who was locked in a freezing latrine all night smeared in her own shit and forced to eat it because she soiled her bed. "Listen," Ivan says to his brother in a kind of fever, "if everyone must suffer, in order to buy eternal harmony with their suffering, pray tell me what have children got to do with it?" Even if one grants, for the sake of argument, that we're all sinners, Ivan wants to know, "what solidarity in sin do little children have? And if it is really true that they, too, are in solidarity with their fathers in all the fathers' evildoings, that truth certainly is not of this world and is incomprehensible to me." Ivan rejects any "higher harmony"—any promise of ultimate truth or salvation, any utopian vision—if it requires the torture and murder of innocents: "They have put too high a price on harmony; we can't afford to pay so much for admission. . . . It's not that I don't accept God, Alyosha, I just most respectfully return him the ticket."

If Ivan's "great sin" is his "rebellion" against the Christian God (or one twisted conception of it, anyway) and his embrace of moral anarchy, then what of Dostoevsky? What were his sins? He was famously conscious of his own status as a "sinner," maybe even a "great" one. He was depressive and suffered at times severe anxiety, and we know about his terrible moods, his irascibility and explosive—though not, it seems, physically violent—outbursts. We know about his compulsive gambling and how it drove the long-suffering Anna, his young second wife, to the edge of despair. (Hers is a remarkable story, recently told by Andrew D. Kaufman in *The Gambler Wife*.) We also know that he was tormented by religious doubt; after all, Ivan K. and his "Legend of the Grand Inquisitor" were always too convincing. More than anything, though, if I were to be the judge, Dostoevsky's "great sin" resembled Ivan's—a sin of intellectual pride, of a morally bankrupt ideology, and most of all, the exertion of a murderous influence.

As his fame grew in the 1870s, Dostoevsky launched a surprisingly successful one-man monthly journal called *A Writer's Diary*, in which he let it all hang out: his post-Siberia conversion to tsarism (reformist, naturally), his aggressive Russian Orthodox Christian nationalism (he beat the drums for an imperialist war against the Turks), and perhaps most damning of all, his antisemitism, ascribing the decline of Europe to the materialistic influence of Jews, "Yids," and decrying a creeping "Yiddism" that supposedly threatened Russia. These opinions, far from being confined to private correspondence (though there's that, too), were paraded in print at the height of his popularity, in the most widely read journalism of his career and as he was gaining access and influence within the royal family itself. Responding defensively (and, tellingly, at great length) to offended Jewish readers in the March 1877 issue of the *Diary*, he claimed that his use of the term "Yiddism" referred to a broad social phenomenon, a tendency of the time, by no means restricted to Jews, and that he directed no hatred toward the Jewish people. Really?

It's impossible to reconcile this late-career Dostoevsky with the Christian-humanistic ideal of universal love at the heart of *The Brothers Karamazov*—which, amazingly, was conceived during those same years. He seems to have been as demoniacally divided within himself, in ways he may not even have understood, as any of his most disturbing (and disturbed) characters. The best that can be said is that Dostoevsky, in his last and greatest literary work, couldn't help but contradict and subvert, consciously or not, his own worst ideological instincts.

If that sounds too easy, too convenient, then look closely at the unexpectedly complex figure of Alyosha—too easily written off as a kind of two-dimensional picture of piety—who explicitly embodies Dostoevsky's Christian-humanist ideal and his hope for Russia's future, and who is, after all, presented as the novel's protagonist. There are two things worth noticing. The first is a conspicuous absence of any nationalist politics—or any Orthodox exclusivity, for that matter—in Alyosha's character. He is remarkably free of xenophobic bigotry or theological dogma and sectarianism; he favors a living, tangible, earthy ethics; he sees and cares about people as people, not theological or ideological constructs. And the second, as emphasized throughout the novel, is Alyosha's steadfast refusal to condemn anyone: not his brute of a father, who abused his devout and doomed mother (she dies when he's a child), and not the atheist-nihilist Ivan. Alyosha seems to grasp intuitively the distinction between judgment and condemnation. He knows it's one thing to judge an action as immoral or criminal, to call a sin a sin, but another thing entirely to condemn a person as irredeemable. It's the latter that Alyosha, under the tutelage of Zosima, refuses to do.

The refusal to condemn—is that what forgiveness is? Not to justify or condone the wrongdoing; not to say, "No problem, we're good, it's okay." But to say: "Actually, it's not okay, and yet despite your crime, despite the harm you've caused, for which you must be held accountable, I still accept you as a fellow human being. Because I, too, am capable of causing suffering, even willfully, if I'm honest. I, too, am a sinner. Our sins may be very different, but I accept your flawed humanity because it's my own."

I can't help wanting Dostoevsky, the human being, to live up to the best ideals of his art. But given what we know, and was easily known to his contemporary readers, about Dostoevsky's political passions and bigotries—and no matter how much the Christlike Alyosha may subvert his author's own darkest obsessions—there will always be something hollow and unconvincing in the Christian-humanistic vision of *The Brothers Karamazov*. As a profession of faith, it is a hollow testament.

Then again, so are most professions of Christianity. It's hard, if not impossible, to escape inconsistency or hypocrisy in any expression of a moral-ethical ideal—thus the convenient escape of cynicism and amorality. And yet even a hypocrite, even a great sinner, can write something true.

"Brothers," says the Elder Zosima, "love man also in his sin, for this likeness of God's love is the height of love on earth."

4. Forgiveness

My father was born in July 1932 in the little town of Blossom, Texas, just east of Paris, the fifth of six children. His parents were tenant farmers, sharecroppers, day laborers. I never knew them; they died too young. That's what poverty does.

The paternal family name was Stefensky or Stefanski (it's not clear which) before his great-grandparents arrived, in 1881, from what is now the Czech Republic. He was the first in his family history to get a college degree, went off to Abilene Christian in 1949, worked in the oil fields to pay for it. He met my mother, a classmate there at Abilene, and got married at age eighteen; got drafted upon graduation; got his master's degree in accounting at the University of Texas on the GI Bill. The rest, to those who knew him, is the stuff of legend. In 1966, two years before I was born, he followed a job out to LA, his wife and three young girls in tow—and that Texas farm boy was off to the races. He built a successful small company and sent his boy to Harvard. Not that he took much interest in the substance of a Harvard education—not until I wrote my thesis on James Agee and *Let Us Now Praise Famous Men*. I think it was Agee's title that appealed to him.

He never went back to those little towns where he grew up, except for rare visits. I went there with him a couple of times, most memorably in 1999, when I made a two-week solo road trip around Texas in search of my roots, four months before my son, our first child, was born. Daddy met me in Paris for two days, and we explored the country church cemeteries and found the old family home places down the dusty back roads. He told me that trip to Paris was one of the best trips of his life—and this was a man who'd been to Paris, France, multiple times.

Over the years I've made several trips back there on my own, the last time in 2016, when I drove up from Nacogdoches after a speaking gig. When I got to the old home place near Mt. Olive, just north of Blossom, now part of a subdivision—the home place where Daddy spent the best years of his boyhood, the years he told me stories about—I found, as I knew someday I would, that what was left of the small ruin of a farmhouse had finally been cleared away, and I walked around the spot where the house had been, now marked by an island of tall grass and wildflowers. But not everything was gone: the tall pine tree his own daddy, Hank, had planted off the front steps of the house was still standing, in spite of a long gash in the trunk where rot had set in.

Daddy never said much about Hank. He talked more about his mother, Lena Josephine—Josie—who raised six children in poverty. All I know is that Hank, in addition to farming, was a carpenter, did construction, day jobs, whatever he could get, and was often away for long stretches looking for work. One of my aunts told me he liked to drink and had a temper, but she didn't say anything more, and I couldn't bring myself to ask.

That Christmas in Nashville, I gave Daddy a few small pieces of bark from Hank's tree and a few bits of cotton I'd picked up by the side of a field south of Blossom, around Biardstown, where his parents farmed "on shares" in the early years of the Depression. It was one of the few times I ever saw him tear up. He always said he could remember his mother pulling him behind her on a cotton sack as she picked cotton—hard, backbreaking labor—under the northeast Texas sun.

§

The last time I saw him, three days after my mother died, it was in the small lobby of the assisted-living home—that was as far as I could enter, like a prison visitation. I'd brought the paperwork from the funeral home for him to sign. We both wore masks, of course, and he had trouble keeping his over his nose. He was far frailer than I'd ever seen him, and quieter. When I got up to leave, we shook hands, and I patted him gently on his stooping back—and I told him, for some unknowable reason, that I'd be there for him, too, as I was for Mother, if there was any way I could. As he turned to go, he paused and looked at me, his mask off. The flesh hung loosely on his face, and his mouth, lips pale, bloodless, made a half smile, half grimace, and in his eyes there was something unmistakably like fear.

Early in the spring he got vaccinated, as did my sister and niece, so that they could visit him. I wouldn't be fully vaccinated until the first week of June, exactly a year after my mother had died, but I went ahead and booked my trip to go see him as soon as I'd be cleared. Then, early in the morning on the last day of May, my sister called to tell me he was gone. He had died, unexpectedly, in the night. She'd been with him the day before, and we were both glad of that. But he never heard me say that I forgave him.

Did I? I don't know. Is this essay my retribution or forgiveness? Maybe it was never up to me to forgive him, maybe that's up to "God," whatever that word means. Maybe there are things that are too much to ask of a child. Maybe it was all I could do, all that could be reasonably asked, just to love him. Not as a child has every desire and every right to love a father—that had long since been impossible—but as a Christian, no, sorry, as any decent human being loves another. Could I love him, as a brother, as a fellow sufferer, a fellow sinner? That's the only question that ever mattered. Can I judge the crime—and still love the man?

5. Brothers

As the brothers face each other in the tavern, Alyosha asks Ivan how his Legend of the Grand Inquisitor comes to an end. The Inquisitor, you may remember, is Dostoevsky's fictional embodiment of what Simone Weil would later call the "totalitarian spirituality" of a church that yields to the third temptation of Christ in the desert: absolute worldly power. Ivan replies, describing the scene in the prison cell as Jesus (if that's who he is) faces the old man who burns heretics in his name:

> [W]hen the Inquisitor fell silent, he waited some time for his prisoner to reply. His silence weighed on him. . . . The old man would have liked him to say something, even something bitter, terrible. But suddenly he approaches the old man in silence and gently kisses him on his bloodless, ninety-year-old lips. That is the whole answer. The old man shudders. . . . "Go and do not come again . . ."

Minutes later, when Alyosha asks Ivan if he still holds to the idea that "everything is permitted," Ivan answers with feeling: "I thought, brother, that when I left here I'd have you, at least, in all the world . . . but now I see that in your heart, too, there is no room for me, my dear hermit. The formula, 'everything is permitted,' I will not renounce, and what then?"

"Alyosha stood up," Dostoevsky writes, "went over to him in silence, and gently kissed him on the lips.

"'Literary theft!' Ivan cried, suddenly going into some kind of rapture."

SEVEN

The Rebel

Camus and the Revolt Against Nihilism

SEPTEMBER 2022

What counts is no longer respecting or sparing a mother's suffering; what counts is securing the victory of a doctrine. And human pain is no longer an outrage, but just a figure on a bill whose dreadful total is not yet calculable.
—Albert Camus, "The Crisis of Man" (1946)

There was a time, perhaps as recently as 2020, when I could still persuade myself, if I really wanted to, that there were arguments for resisting despair of my country and world. I still believed, or wanted to believe, that there was a chance, however slim, to turn things around politically before the clock ran down on our converging crises of democracy, social and economic injustice, and climate catastrophe. This was back when something like a comprehensive climate, jobs, and social policy framework still appeared at the outer edge of the possible, so that, the thinking went, with enough pressure from a coalition of emboldened social movements we might actually, not *solve* our compounding emergencies at one stroke, but at least, maybe, turn the tide.

This was before the precipitous downward spiral of American democracy was an established fact; before the brazen lie of a stolen election and the cynical manipulation by elites of an armed white-nationalist movement itching to kill in Jesus's name; before a maniacal Oval Office cabal conspired to violently obstruct the constitutional transfer of power and before the murderous assault on the Capitol led by neofascist militias embraced by the Republican Party. It was before a Supreme Court packed by that same authoritarian party stripped half the population of fundamental bodily autonomy and bent the Constitution to serve criminally reckless corporate interests in guns and oil. It was before the so-called reasonable adults in the Democratic Party controlling Congress and the White House allowed the carbon lobby to eviscerate the only legislation in three decades that might help slow the accelerating climate breakdown—at the cost of countless lives, the vast majority among the global poor and marginalized—and the climate movement celebrated it as a victory. And it was before the slide into electoral chaos. Before all the talk of civil war.

There are professional optimists, ingenuous merchants of magical thinking, who treat other people's despair as either irrational catastrophism or, among activists, a kind of moral defect—as if despair is a matter of just *not trying* hard enough, *not caring* enough, rather than a natural and entirely sane human response to empirical reality. I refuse to apologize or seek forgiveness for my despair in the face of plain facts, scientific and political, or to condemn others for theirs. My despair is not the sort that says, fatalistically, there's nothing left to be done, and walks away. If only it were so simple. There's much to be done—if only to salvage what we as humans can, and to survive.

And yet, there's something about despair that the hope-mongers may indeed grasp, something I've sensed viscerally for a long time. Despair is dangerous. Not in itself a character flaw or moral failing, it can nevertheless lead to some very dark places. And so, even as I accept my condition and the facts of our situation, there's a question that—as an engaged citizen and as a human being who doesn't want to give up on human beings—won't let me rest: What follows despair?

If despair is an experience one passes through, a frontier one crosses, what's on the other side? Is there nothing but an endless wasteland of fatalism, meaningless futility—a chilling, inevitable nihilism? If all dreams of a "better world" for generations to come have died—if all that's left is the brute, life-or-death struggle for power and survival, rationalized and sanctified by cynical ideologies of "us" and "them," "freedom" and "justice," or whatever you choose—then what's to keep me, in the midst of such a world, from becoming that which I've long rejected and struggled against? What's to keep me from joining those who abstract and dehumanize the enemy, the collective other, and meet fear with fear, hate with hate, violence with violence?

So, yes, if I'm honest, I'll admit that my despair scares me. I can try to ignore it, distract myself, pretend it's not there or that it will somehow go away, but the truth is I'm constantly aware of its dark gravitational pull, drawing me toward a desolation in which anything might happen—in which the perceived imperatives of the historical moment and the rationalizations of ends and means might justify anything, any price, any sacrifice, mine or another's.

Against this fear, I can only ask myself, is there still something within me, here on the other side of despair, with the power to resist the cold undertow of nihilism? I still cling to the belief that there must be. But what is it? And whatever name I give it, how do I know it's real?

§

It's safe to say that Albert Camus was on intimate terms with despair.

Maybe this is why I find myself returning to him again and again. Because, along with other members of his European generation—Hannah Arendt and Simone Weil, as we've seen, to name just two—he witnessed, and in some ways personally experienced, the worst of what humanity could do, and yet, he emerged in search of reasons not to give up on human beings. It wouldn't be easy—indeed, for Camus and others it felt as if they must start from zero.

"The years we have gone through have killed something in us," Camus wrote in "Neither Victims Nor Executioners," in November 1946. Gone, he wrote, was "the old confidence man had in himself, which led him to believe that he could always elicit human reactions from another man if he spoke to him in the language of a common humanity." This was no longer possible, he contended, "because one cannot appeal to an abstraction, i.e., the representative of an ideology."

That series of eight brief essays—analyzing and diagnosing the moral-political illness of his European century—ran on the front page of *Combat*, the important French Resistance newspaper for which Camus had written and served as editor in chief, both before the Liberation (when it was a high-risk underground operation) and after. He was responding, in large part, to the immediate postwar political crisis in France and the messy purge of Vichy collaborationists. Having initially endorsed the death penalty for leading collaborators and perpetrators of atrocities, he soon recoiled in disgust as the trials and executions turned into an opportunistic partisan bloodletting.

In this atmosphere of fear and violence—both the fear of a new East–West war and, he wrote, "the specific fear of murderous ideologies"—Camus perceived something essential. "We live in terror because persuasion is no longer possible," he wrote, "because we live in a world of abstractions, of bureaus and machines, of absolute ideas and of crude messianism." In the ideologies of both right and left he found the dehumanizing, fatalistic logic of "a world where murder is legitimate." And so Camus announced that he had reached a decision and stated it for the record—an act which, Camus being among the most widely read and respected journalists in France, was sure to turn heads. "I will never again be one of those, whoever they be, who compromise with murder," he told his readers, adding, "I must take the consequences of such a decision." (It was enough to catch the eye of a kindred spirit on the other side of the Atlantic, Dwight Macdonald, who published his own translation of the series, which I'm quoting here, in the July–August 1947 issue of *Politics*.)

"All I ask is that, in the midst of a murderous world, we agree to reflect on murder and to make a choice," Camus wrote in a final, bracing paragraph that still echoes (well served by Macdonald's elegant phrasings). "After that," he coolly observed, "we can distinguish those who accept the consequences of being murderers themselves or the accomplices of murderers, and those who refuse to do so with all their force and being. Since this terrible dividing line does exist, it will be a gain if it be clearly marked."

The ideas in "Neither Victims Nor Executioners" had been percolating and surfacing in Camus's work for many months, stretching back into the war years, and were coalescing into the major themes of his epochal debate with contemporaries on the left. That debate culminated in Camus's book-length essay *The Rebel* in 1951 (the same year that Arendt's *Origins of Totalitarianism* appeared, as well as Weil's *Waiting for God*, published by Camus at Gallimard), which marked his definitive break with Communist and fellow-travelling intellectuals, most famously his erstwhile friend Sartre. And perhaps Camus's first major sketch of these themes, still well worth reading, was the lecture he gave at Columbia University on March 28, 1946, called "The Crisis of Man" (included in the recent Vintage collection *Speaking Out: Lectures and Speeches*,

1937–1958, translated by Quintin Hoare).

The Columbia lecture also takes a prominent place in the humanities scholar Robert Meagher's recent study, *Albert Camus and the Human Crisis*. Meagher, an emeritus professor at Hampshire College who taught a popular course on Camus—and is on a personal mission to shore up Camus's humanist universalism against more recent intellectual currents—offers many useful insights, even if the book verges on hagiography. For instance, it seems important to point out, as Meagher does, that in "The Crisis of Man," Camus "distilled in twenty-two minutes his life and work"—and to note that his Columbia hosts, at a time when American readers only knew Camus's early books *The Stranger* and *The Myth of Sisyphus* (both published in 1942), "had invited an existentialist and found themselves confronted by a moralist." As Meagher notes, Camus adamantly rejected the "existentialist" label. In the words of philosopher William Barrett (quoted by Meagher), Camus was "the advocate of what he came to call 'ordinary values'—those elementary feelings of common decency without which the human race would not survive."

That spring of 1946, Camus was still at work on his next novel, *The Plague* (1947), and in "The Crisis of Man" he delineated the symptoms of the scourge he saw afflicting European civilization in the twentieth century—summed up as "the worship of both efficiency and abstraction." Most of all, the crisis could be seen in the replacement of actual human beings with "political man," as defined entirely by "collective passions—in other words, abstract passions." Lost in the bargain was something basic: "What counts is no longer respecting or sparing a mother's suffering; what counts is securing the victory of a doctrine."

Camus went on in the lecture to interpret the experience of those in his generation who, like himself, realized that they lacked something vital, something essential to the task of resisting the total-itarian plague. "The more aware among us," he said, "perceived that they did not yet have, in the realm of thought, any principle which might allow them to oppose terror and repudiate murder." And he continued:

> For if you basically believe in nothing, if nothing has any meaning and we can proclaim no value, then everything is allowed, and nothing is important. Then there is neither good nor evil, and Hitler was neither wrong nor right. You can send millions of innocent people to the gas chamber just as you can dedicate yourself to caring for lepers.

Logic, in itself, whether in the pseudoscience of racial destiny or dialectical materialism, would never suffice. "Nihilism," Camus observed, "has been replaced by absolute rationalism and in both cases the results are the same. . . . [A]ll acts are justified not insofar as they are good or bad, but insofar as they are effective or not."

These lines contain glimmers, and more than glimmers, of both *The Plague* and *The Rebel*, the main pillars of what Camus considered the second stage of his work; in the first (*The Stranger*, *The Myth of Sisyphus*, and his play *Caligula*), he established negation and the absurd, now followed by affirmation and revolt. "It was quite useless to tell us, 'You must believe in God, or Plato, or Marx,' because we precisely did not have that kind of faith," he explained to his New York audience:

> This is why we sought a reason in our revolt itself. . . . We said "no" to that world, to its essential absurdity, to the ab-stractions which threatened us, to the civilization of death being prepared for us. By saying "no" we affirmed that

things had gone on long enough; that there was a limit which could not be crossed. . . . we affirmed that there was something in us which rejected what was outrageous, and which could no longer be humiliated. . . . And consequently, by the very fact of living, hoping and struggling, we were all affirming something.

In the midst of nihilistic terror—family, neighbors, comrades tortured, lined up and shot, deported to the camps—"we were in a collective tragedy," Camus observed, "where what was at stake was a common dignity, a shared human communion, which had to be defended and maintained."

§

On January 22, 1956, the shouts of "Death to Camus!" could be heard from violent "ultracolonialists" outside the Cercle du Progrès in Algiers, where the famous French Algerian writer had come to deliver his "Appeal for a Civilian Truce." Camus had long been a consistent and formidable critic of the French colonial regime, advocating justice for the Arab and Berber peoples of Algeria since the late 1930s, when as a young left-wing journalist he wrote a damning exposé of extreme poverty and inequality in Kabylia for the anticolonialist *Alger républicain* (leading to the paper's official censoring and closing and his own de facto exile to France). But that day in 1956 he stood virtually alone among French intellectuals on the left, who had more recently taken up the Algerian cause, as he came home to a bloody, war-torn Algiers and organized, at no small risk, an idealistic (some would say quixotic) effort to secure an agreement between the French forces and the Front de Libération Nationale (FLN) to cease the targeting of civilians by both sides.

Addressing a mostly friendly audience inside the hall that day, Camus explained that he'd called the meeting—attended by representatives of the dwindling moderate factions and various religious communities, Muslim and Christian—in order to offer "a purely human appeal" and to demonstrate "at least that all chance of dialogue is not lost." The speech, which is also included in the Vintage collection, is well known to students of Camus. (It also appears in the indispensable 2013 edition of Camus's *Algerian Chronicles* edited by Alice Kaplan and translated by Arthur Goldhammer.) And it's worth revisiting, perhaps especially right now, as a critical moment in the story of Camus's moral and political engagement with his time and place.

"My sole qualification for intervening on this issue," Camus told his audience, "is to have experienced the Algerian misfortune as a personal tragedy." Camus was no bourgeois colonialist—he grew up in a working-class *pied noir* family (in Algeria for three generations), subsisting on what his war-widow mother earned cleaning houses and his bachelor uncle's wages in a cooper's shop. His primary reason for issuing the appeal was not political or tactical but "purely humanitarian," he insisted. "Whatever the long-standing, deep-seated origins of the Algerian tragedy, one fact remains: no cause justifies the death of innocents." For Camus, on an intellectual (and no less personal) level, the moment was inseparable from the philosophical and moral questions he had wrestled with throughout his life and writing, from wartime resistance to postwar reckoning and his lonely and very public break with fellow leftists over Stalinism.

Among the most urgent of those questions for Camus was the possibility of any genuine communication, understanding, and ultimately, solidarity, based on the recognition of common human values, a "common humanity." If the Algerian violence descended into a "xenophobic frenzy," Camus warned, "then all chance of understanding would be drowned definitively in blood." Such "horrors" may have already been unleashed, he acknowledged, speaking five months after the Philippeville massacre of *pied noir* civilians and the vastly disproportionate reprisals by the French. "But that must not and cannot happen," he argued, "without those among us, Arab and French, who reject the madness and destruction of nihilism, issuing one last appeal to reason."

"People resign themselves too easily to fatality," Camus observed—while Frenchmen shouted for his death on the streets outside. "They accept too easily the idea that blood alone moves history forward. . . . This fatality does perhaps exist. But the task of men is not to accept it, nor to submit to its laws."

Camus's initiative, which even friends quietly considered out of touch with the realities on the ground, went nowhere (and became something of a joke among his smirking Parisian critics). And so Camus, defeated and despairing, fell silent—both from a sense of futility and a fear of only inflaming passions with his words and thus contributing to the violence. But he never turned his back on Algeria, as many accused him. As he told the audience that day in 1956, "I have loved with passion this land in which I was born; I have drawn from her everything that I am." His mother and relatives still lived in the Belcourt neighborhood of Algiers where he grew up, and he still visited. And he continued to work behind the scenes, advocating for the lives of condemned political prisoners, including Algerian nationalists, with some success.

So it was that nearly two years later, on December 12, 1957, Camus stood before a group of university students at a press conference in Stockholm, where he had accepted the Nobel Prize in Literature two days prior and found himself confronted by a young Algerian nationalist in the crowd who heatedly pressed him to justify his long silence. As reported by *Le Monde*'s Dominique Birmann (apparently the only French reporter to file a dispatch), in what Alice Kaplan aptly calls a "tragicomedy of misquotation," Camus's generous reply would be remembered only for Birmann's inept paraphrase (to put it kindly) of Camus's provocative remark: "I have always condemned terror. I must also condemn the blind terrorism that can be seen in the streets of Algiers, for example, which someday might strike my mother or family. I believe in justice, but I will defend my mother before justice." Kaplan notes that polemicists further distorted the final sentence, which was repeated in the press as: "Between justice and my mother, I choose my mother." ("I was totally sure that Camus would say some fucking fool thing," said *Le Monde*'s director, Hubert Beuve-Méry.)

What Camus really said, according to both Kaplan and biographer Olivier Todd (based on an interview with Camus's translator Carl-Gustav Bürstrom, who was present), was this: "People are now planting bombs in the tramways of Algiers. My mother might be on one of those tramways. If that is justice, then I prefer my mother." In other words, if your concept of justice included the indiscriminate murder of ordinary civilians, Camus was not your ally.

The following June, Gallimard came out with *Actuelles III: Chroniques algériennes, 1939–1958* (simply *Algerian Chronicles* in English), a collection of Camus's reporting, essays, and speeches on Algeria, together with a new preface and concluding chapter that would be his final words on the conflict. Clearly exasperated by the polemicists, he made sure in his preface that there could be no doubt as to where he stood. He decried the "casuistry of blood" with which each side "justifies its own actions by pointing to the crimes of its adversaries." The terrorist tactics of the FLN, against both French and Arab civilians, should be condemned "in the bluntest of terms," he wrote, obviously addressing his former friends on the left. But

Camus reserved his strongest words for anyone who would try to enlist him as an apologist for the French regime. "The [French] reprisals against the civilian population of Algeria and the use of torture against the rebels are crimes for which we all bear a share of responsibility," Camus wrote. "Meanwhile, we must refuse to justify these methods on any grounds whatsoever, including effectiveness. Once one begins to justify them, even indirectly, no rules or values remain. One cause is as good as another, and pointless warfare, unrestrained by the rule of law, consecrates the triumph of nihilism."

§

If you've read "The Crisis of Man" and "Neither Victims Nor Executioners," then the opening pages of *The Rebel* have a familiar ring, as Camus memorably states his case, now refined and polished to a high aphoristic gloss. "We shall know nothing," he writes, "until we know whether we have the right to kill our fellow men. . . . In the age of ideologies, we must examine our position in relation to murder. . . . Each day at dawn, assassins in judges' robes slip into some cell. . . . Thus, whichever way we turn, in our abyss of negation and nihilism, murder has its privileged position." Of the inherent human affirmation he found in the act of revolt, Camus now writes, "When he rebels, a man identifies himself with other men. . . . Man's solidarity is founded upon rebellion, and rebellion, in its turn, can only find its justification in this solidarity." Any revolutionary movement, then, that denies this fundamental human solidarity can no longer be called rebellion, as Camus defines it, but instead "becomes in reality an acquiescence in murder." Camus never renounced the violence of the Resistance—he was not an absolute pacifist—because it was a rebellion in defense of that human solidarity and against totalitarian nihilism.

Camus knew his readers, and he knew that his critique of the logic of ends and means, by which their political commitments were justified, still left the question of ultimate value or any transcendent moral truth unresolved. Not that Camus ever reached a final answer himself, or ever claimed to—on the contrary, he maintained an admirable intellectual humility in an age of absolutes. And yet, deep in the final section of *The Rebel*, where he does battle with Marxist historical determinism, he dangles a tantalizing remark, drawing on older moral-philosophical resources, hinting at a way out of the impasse. "Does the end justify the means?" he asks. "That is possible. But what will justify the end? To that question, which historical thought leaves pending, rebellion replies: the means."

This is no mere glib tautology. I'd suggest that it points to what social movement thinkers might call a "prefigurative" politics—the notion that movements for justice and democracy need to represent and embody the values and principles of the world they want to create. A movement that devalues human life and legitimizes premeditated murder will, if and when it takes power, only further legitimize a murderous world. If our struggles for democracy, justice, and human rights rely on antidemocratic, unjust, and inhuman methods and tactics, then whatever we achieve will be corrupted and ultimately false.

This would seem to be Camus's most basic gut check. He would simply have us ask ourselves, engaging in the kind of self-questioning that Arendt saw in those who refuse to go along with evil: If I achieve these ends by these means, will I still be able to live with myself and others? Or will I have betrayed whatever it is that allows me to communicate and to live in community with other human beings?

§

"Now the street was experiencing the liveliness of a Sunday morning,"

Camus writes in *The First Man*, the unfinished autobiographical novel he left behind at his death in a car accident in January 1960. His fictional self, Jacques Cormery, is sitting in his elderly mother's apartment in Algiers looking down at the working-class neighborhood he knew so well as a child. It's the late 1950s, and paratroopers patrol the streets. "Workingmen in freshly washed and ironed white shirts were chatting on their way to the three or four cafés, which smelled of cool shade and anise," he writes. "Some Arabs were passing by, poor also but decently dressed. . . . Now and then entire Arab families went by in their Sunday best."

And then, out of nowhere, an explosion—"very close, enormous"—at a busy trolley stop down the street:

> His mother had recoiled to the back of the room, pale, her dark eyes full of a fear she could not control, and she was unsteady on her feet. 'It's here. It's here,' she was saying.

Jacques goes down to the street. Men are shouting:

> 'That filthy race,' a short worker in an undershirt said, looking in the direction of an Arab. . . . 'I didn't do anything,' the Arab said. 'You're all in it together, all you fucking sons of bitches,' and he started toward him.

Jacques takes the Arab into a nearby café run by a childhood friend, who shelters him. Back outside, Jacques tells the scowling worker: "He hasn't done anything." The worker replies: "We should kill them all."

Back in the apartment, Jacques sits down with his mother and holds her hands:

'Twice this week,' she said. 'I'm afraid to go out . . . I'm old. I can't run anymore . . .' 'Come with me to France,' he said to her, but she shook her head with resolute sorrow. 'Oh no, it's cold over there. I'm too old now. I want to stay home.'

The scenes are fictional, but entirely plausible. In his 1958 preface to *Algerian Chronicles*, Camus minces no words when it comes to the heavy price being paid by civilians, Arab and Berber and French. And as he reminds his readers, on this question the political was for him intensely personal. "I am recounting the story of my own family, which, being poor and devoid of hatred, never exploited or oppressed anyone," he writes. "But three-quarters of the French in Algeria are like my relatives."

Independence on the FLN's terms, Camus notes, would mean the expulsion of a French Algerian population of more than a million people. Fully acknowledging "the end of colonialism," Camus excludes "any thought of reconquest or continuation of the status quo." And yet, he writes, "I also rule out any thought of uprooting the French of Algeria, who do not have the right to oppress anyone but do have the right not to be oppressed themselves, as well as the right to determine their own future in the land of their birth." In a piece for *L'Express*, where he wrote a column in 1955 and 1956, Camus points out that the minimum wage for French Algerian workers, although unjustly higher than that of Arabs, was lower than in the poorest parts of France. "Those are your colonial profiteers," he dryly notes. Why, he asks, must these struggling workers and their families "be sacrificed to expiate the immense sins of French colonization?" To be clear, he states, "The Arabs are due a major reparation, in my opinion, a stunning reparation. But it must come from France as a whole, not from the blood of French men and women living in Algeria."

Sartre, in his 1961 introduction to Frantz Fanon's *The Wretched of the Earth*, swooned over Fanon's cold-blooded analysis of anticolonial violence as a creative and (in Sartre's reading) therapeutic force—to the point of exaggerating and romanticizing Fanon's bloodiness, no doubt in an effort to shock the sensibilities of polite French liberals. The "irrepressible violence" of the colonized is nothing less, in Sartre's telling, than "man reconstructing himself." In their uncontrollable "rage," the colonized "recover their lost coherence, they experience self-knowledge." (Reading it today in the recent anniversary edition, one catches, ironically enough, more than a whiff of Orientalist exoticism in Sartre's enthusiasm for the seductive, primal bloodlust of the "native.") Throughout this orgy of murderous abstraction, Sartre never distinguishes between combatants and civilians, much less between capitalists and workers—no European is innocent, all are equally complicit in the fraud of Western humanist ideals. "The pacifists are a fine sight: neither victims nor torturers! Come now! . . . your passiveness serves no other purpose but to put you on the side of the oppressors." It seems the philosophe couldn't resist one parting cut at Camus's corpse. (An unjust cut—Camus, as we've seen, was far from passive toward Algeria.)

For Sartre, writing about Fanon from Paris, "killing a European"—note, any European—"is killing two birds with one stone, eliminating in one go oppressor and oppressed: leaving one man dead and the other free." I'm sorry, but if that is your idea of justice, then I, too, prefer Camus's mother.

Some still like to paint Camus as a liberal individualist and a Western imperialist-colonialist. The truth is, he was always a man of the left (briefly a Communist in his early years in Algeria), but he was an anti-totalitarian socialist—one reason Dwight Macdonald and Hannah Arendt admired him—even what we might call a *democratic* socialist. And he simply could not bring himself to support

Algerian independence at *any and all cost*. He was never going to use his voice to justify crimes against humanity—whether revolutionary terror against civilians or mass ethnic cleansing—in order to prove his anti-imperialist bona fides to the French intellectual left.

Yes, a white, male, European "settler" denying a colonized people the moral right to achieve liberation by *any means* necessary—one can't help but cringe, these days, to be sure. It's one thing when he's opposing Nazi and Stalinist terror. It feels different, and uncomfortably closer to home in our current moment, when he's opposing a liberationist movement's revolutionary violence against a Western colonial power. But is it really all that different? Camus forces us to think about fundamental principles: Is "everything permitted" in the cause of what we call justice, freedom, liberation—or only, perhaps, in our own ideologically approved cases?

If the descent of our tech-mediated and increasingly violent political discourse to new lows of religious, racial, and ideological tribalism is any indication, there are a great many people today—all across the political spectrum—who seem to have traded any respect of actual human beings for abstract, collective passions. One fears, in the dehumanization of our politics, that nihilism is winning. If, for now, its advances are confined mostly to the right, that's little reason for comfort. As Camus saw, it spreads like a virus.

§

There's a scene in *The Plague* on which the whole novel hinges, and it's what you could call a showstopper. (I had to put the book down and take a break after reading it for the first time years ago.) The humanitarian physician, Dr. Rieux, and members of his citizen plague-fighting team, including the aging priest, Father Paneloux, are watching the death throes of a child who has been given a serum that might save his life but in the end only prolongs the boy's unspeakable suffering—described by Camus in meticulous, harrowing detail. "They had already seen children die, since terror, for months now, came at random," Camus writes (in Laura Marris's translation),

> but they had never yet followed a child's suffering minute after minute as they had been doing since the early hours. And to them, of course, the pain inflicted on these innocents had always seemed like what it truly was—a scandal. But at least up until then, in some ways it had scandalized them in the abstract, because they had never stared directly, for so long, at the agony of an innocent.

Later, outside the ward, Dr. Rieux speaks passionately with Father Paneloux, with whom he has carried on an almost Dostoevskian debate about God, meaningless suffering, and evil. But unlike Camus's Meursault in *The Stranger* (the doctor's absurdist predecessor), Rieux finds a kind of solidarity with the clergyman, whose faith is shaken but still holds, and responds to him with compassion. Rieux can never share Paneloux's belief, he makes that clear, but he assures him nevertheless, "We're working for something that brings us together beyond blasphemies and prayers. It's all that matters."

§

What's on the other side of despair? Only the world, just as it is and has always been. Nothing more, nothing less. Pointless suffering, yes. Cruelty and injustice, yes. Nihilistic rationalizations of violence, of murder, yes. And yet, too: Revolt. Solidarity. Love (another name for revolt and solidarity). Not in the abstract, but living, breathing, bleeding, human. The same as they ever were but somehow clearer now: the only ends and means worth living for.

PART THREE

On the Other Side
of Despair

EIGHT

How to Blow Up a Climate Fantasy

Against Climate Optimism

DECEMBER 2022; APRIL 2023

1.

Ten days after the 2022 midterm elections, Liz Cheney, the anti-MAGA yet deeply conservative outgoing congresswoman from Wyoming, may have said it best: The election results were "a clear victory for team normal." The center held. "Democracy," such as it is, held. Even stalwart progressive comrades of mine in the climate movement found the results reassuring. And it's true, full control of the Senate would help the Democrats defend their legislative gains. But even if they had managed to hold the House as well, US climate policy—at both the national and global level—would remain far behind where it needs to be.

At the same time, yet another UN climate conference—the 27th—produced little or no progress on global emissions. The goal of limiting warming to 1.5 degrees Celsius hangs by a thread. So let's be clear: If there's going to be the slightest chance of salvaging the now all-but-defunct Paris Agreement goal of averting catastrophe for a vast portion of humanity, overwhelmingly in the Global South—catastrophe that is already underway—something will have to give.

A great many words have been written (including by me) about reasons for political and climate despair—the two are inseparable—and reasons to resist them. And along with the postelection relief at a seeming return to political "normalcy," there's an equally premature sense of optimism among climate pundits and movement insiders—as though recent progress has bought us some breathing room. A sense that we might finally be *winning*.

It may be true, as David Wallace-Wells reported in *The New York Times Magazine* (in what is probably the year's most influential piece of climate writing), that thanks to scientists' revised climate and energy models—plus totally unforeseen technological and economic progress on renewables—humanity has "likely" escaped the very worst-case scenarios. Rather than a "truly apocalyptic" 4- or 5-degrees Celsius warming by 2100, we are now looking at the prospect of a *mere* 2 to 3.5 degrees, based on current policies and pledges (that is, words on paper). This was what most mainstream commentators and interviewers, ever looking for the hopeful spin, took away from Wallace-Wells. But as he went on to point out, given the expected impacts of 2-plus degrees of warming—and the fact that impacts are already far more severe than predicted at just 1.2 degrees—even this lowered estimate will be a very rough ride, especially for those who don't live in the wealthier parts of the Global North. Thus the rising intensity of the demands at COP27—and the surprise baby-steps agreement—for "loss and damage" payments to poor and vulnerable countries already suffering unprecedented extremes.

Such is the case for optimism. Meanwhile, global emissions are still rising. As the IPCC reported back in 2018, in order to have a shot at avoiding 1.5°C, the world's emissions must plummet *by half* by 2030. Newly inked investments in oil and gas projects (some deals apparently made on the sidelines at COP27), profiteering off the energy crisis caused by Russia's invasion of Ukraine, will blow the Paris Agreement carbon budget in less than a decade—despite the International Energy Agency's latest warning that *no new fossil-fuel infrastructure* can be built if the Paris goals are to mean anything. All this bad news (and there's plenty more), even as recent science points to an increasing likelihood of crossing irreversible earth-system "tipping points" between 1.5 and 2°C.

This is what winning looks like—for some people. It's the world, anyway, that "team normal" has given us.

§

There's something deeply disturbing—chilling, even—about the doctrinaire insistence upon hope and optimism in Democratic and mainstream climate movement circles. I find it chilling because it implies, on the part of the optimists (who are, by the way, almost always white, and either NGO- or party-affiliated), a readiness to settle. That is, a readiness to accept a world beyond 1.5 degrees, even 2 degrees—with all that will bring. It's hard to fathom how anyone could accept or resign themselves to such a thing, unless they're already fundamentally comfortable with our political and economic system—the system that got us here—and have faith (however naïve) in its ability, and theirs, to weather the storm. At the very least it reveals an unwillingness to do, or even to consider, what is actually required—to take the necessary risks, individually and collectively, as a movement.

And yet, regardless of the new optimist orthodoxy, there are still quite a few people—and their numbers will grow, I'd wager, as a new generation is radicalized—who are unwilling and, on some visceral level, unable to accept the systemic barbarity of a global ecocide that amounts, in many places on the planet, to a form of genocide: that is, the foreseeable and preventable yet willfully driven decimation of entire populations, even the eradication of whole countries and cultures. Some of us are not willing and able to settle—or to go along with a movement that settles—for genocide.

That's easy to say, of course—mere words. But what do I really mean?

As the internationally agreed-upon goal of 1.5°C is effectively abandoned, the world is well past the point where there's the slimmest chance of averting such eco-/genocide without in fact *shutting things down* that already exist and *stopping new things* from being built. Things like pipelines, coal mines, power plants, drilling rigs, oil and gas export terminals. There are multiple ways of doing this, some of them financial and regulatory—i.e., the normal, business-as-usual ways—and some of them direct.

Why bother with the far riskier—and more forceful—direct ways, skeptics will ask, when there's no guarantee they'll convince "team normal" to abandon business as usual? Here's one answer: because nothing else has worked, and time is up. Nothing has created the sense of crisis necessary to break the grip of those who protect and profit from the status quo.

And here's another, every bit as important: Direct action is a form of truth-telling—maybe the most powerful form of truth-telling that social movements have yet invented. It demonstrates, not in the abstract but physically, bodily, on the ground and at the root, *what needs to be done*—and demonstrates *the will to do it*. The will to place human life, all life, ahead of the interests of corporate property and profit. (I'm speaking here only of what I and others consider nonviolent direct action, that which strictly avoids physically harming other people; corporations are not people, and destruction of corporate property is not violence.) While this kind of action doesn't require massive numbers in order to be effective (though the more the better), it does help considerably if it has the support of aligned social and political movements.

To the shame of the US climate movement, and much of the left more broadly, such support is what's lacking in this moment of utmost need. Since 2020, the US climate movement, at the national level, has if anything *de*mobilized—content to pursue an inside strategy, employing the mildest of tactics, becoming in effect a mere extension of the progressive wing of the Democratic Party.

But those who are committed to the truth-telling of direct action will not go away just because the future looks a little brighter for the comparatively rich people in the Global North—the countries historically responsible for the coming devastation and erasure of entire countries and cultures. They'll do what's necessary, with or without the blessing of a movement that settles.

One reason I think Andreas Malm's 2021 manifesto, *How to Blow Up a Pipeline,* struck such a nerve among climate activists and others on the left (see, for example, the anthology *Property Will Cost Us the Earth,* a collection of responses to Malm) is the way it forces readers to ask themselves, as they look into the abyss—the desolation towards which political normalcy, the status quo, is leading us—what is in fact necessary and morally justified in our situation. What risks are acceptable? At this juncture, as Malm put it when I spoke with him in December 2020, there are "no safe options." He's right. Those of us engaged in the struggle for climate justice must ask ourselves whether sticking with politics and activism as usual, in the face of our global emergency, isn't itself a kind of giving up, a kind of fatalism, even despair.

In which case, perhaps those who are still committed to the radical truth-telling of direct action—who refuse to give their consent to eco-/genocide—are the real optimists. Some might call them optimists of the will. At this late hour, there's no other kind.

2.

On March 20, 2023, the final installment of the Sixth Assessment Report of the Intergovernmental Panel on Climate Change (IPCC) landed with all the force of a pebble hurled into the sea. Another round of dutifully—and accurately—alarming coverage appeared on the world's news pages and in social media feeds, but it was barely acknowledged by the guardians of our political and cultural status quo and their corporate paymasters.

As many have noted, this latest IPCC report contains no new scientific revelations; there is no news to be broken. It is, rather, an elaborate exercise in messaging. And what a feast for the "climate comms" crowd to chew on. In what is surely a first, UN Secretary General António Guterres alluded to this year's Oscar winner for Best Picture, *Everything Everywhere All at Once*, in trying to describe what must be done at this emergency juncture.

But however you dress it up, the salient points remain what we've known for some time:

- The Paris Agreement's goal of limiting warming to 1.5°C above the preindustrial average is all but dead. The planet is now likely to cross that threshold in the early 2030s.
- Some parts of the world are rapidly approaching, or have already reached, the "limits of adaptation" (see: rising sea levels, desertification, and extreme heat intolerable to the human body). With every additional increment of warming, the task of adaptation gets harder and costlier, if not impossible.

- Our only chance at stabilizing the climate requires deep and rapid decarbonization, which entails not only the accelerated build-out of renewable energy but *the immediate end* of all new fossil-fuel development. Even existing coal, oil, and gas operations will blow through the atmospheric "carbon budget" for limiting the planet's warming to 1.5°C—or even 2°C. We must shut them down.
- The developed nations have "sufficient global capital" to invest in drastic decarbonization—if "existing barriers" (the IPCC doesn't name names) are overcome.
- Most important—especially to those for whom sustaining optimism is paramount—the Paris goals are still *technically and economically feasible*, as experts love to say, assuming the viability of "net-negative" emissions techniques (i.e., removing carbon dioxide from the atmosphere), which remain unproven at scale. It's only the political will that's lacking.

Guterres calls the report "a how-to guide to defuse the climate time bomb." But it isn't really. That's because the IPCC says nothing (and never has) about how to overcome those "existing barriers." All we're told is that—ready?—"political commitment" will be required.

The apparently unspeakable truth, for the IPCC and for mainstream journalists and advocates, is the necessity of something like a near-term political revolution to topple those barriers. Yet there's an utter lack of anything remotely resembling the kind of mass political movement capable of bringing it about. The present risk-averse mainstream climate movement certainly isn't; nor is any other force on the left. Even well-informed progressives are more inclined to toil away at incrementalist politics-as-usual—or fantasize about far-off technological breakthroughs (nuclear fusion!)—than face up to the kind of radical "political commitment" that's necessary. To call 1.5°C or 2°C "feasible" in the face of these realities is simply magical thinking.

More than a decade ago, it was widely noted that the Obama–Biden administration's support for the proposed Keystone XL pipeline flew in the face of climate science. The International Energy Agency had by then reached the conclusion that new investments in fossil-fuel infrastructure would have to end by 2017 if warming was to be kept below 2°C. Thanks to years of sustained direct action that galvanized the climate-justice movement, Keystone XL is dead—a historic victory. But as if to show us (and certain donors, no doubt) what he's really made of, just days before the new IPCC report was released, President Biden approved the massive Willow oil project in Alaska's Arctic—even as China significantly expands its use of coal power. And why not? Global emissions reached another record high in 2022. It's simply business as usual. Another word for it is nihilism.

A true reckoning with the radical implications of climate science—that nothing short of political revolution will prevent what amounts to genocide for large, mostly darker-skinned and neocolonized portions of humanity—has yet to come. And yet, in one form or another, a reckoning will come: everywhere, and all at once.

NINE

Risk and Revolution

A Specter Haunts the Climate Left

JULY 2023

The strongest weapon against revolution, or any hankering for it . . . [is] that capitalist-realist common sense that it's impossible, even laughable, to struggle or hope for change.
—China Miéville, *A Spectre, Haunting: On* The Communist Manifesto (2022)

1.

The laughter is the tell. In a deftly written and acted scene in *How to Blow Up a Pipeline*, the action-thriller directed by Daniel Goldhaber (and inspired by Andreas Malm's identically titled 2021 book, which, unlike the film, does not describe how to blow up anything), a ragtag group of eight fossil-fuel saboteurs—young, diverse, mostly working class, several from polluted frontline communities—pass a bottle around, blowing off steam the night before they blow up a pipeline in the West Texas desert.

"They're gonna call us revolutionaries, or game changers," offers Rowan (Kristine Froseth), a waifish blonde anarchist with a smirky grin. Somebody laughs. "No, they'll call us terrorists," says dread-locked, queer Theo (Sasha Lane). And Theo is right. You don't even have to sabotage a pipeline to be called a terrorist in this country—as we've seen in Georgia, where more than forty activists have been charged with "domestic terrorism" for allegedly damaging property and trespassing while protesting Atlanta's "Cop City."

But the laughter captures something else about our political-cultural era. Almost no one takes revolution seriously—not even fictional would-be revolutionaries on screen. And not even in the face of our fossil-fuel driven global emergency. In fact, it would seem the only revolutionaries in this country are found on the far right—as a Proud Boy testified, their goal on Jan. 6, 2021, was "all-out revolution."

Most interesting about Goldhaber's film—which is that rare thing, a politically thoughtful action movie—is the way it dramatizes and draws out the fears and anxieties of climate activism at this stage of the crisis. (Full disclosure: I'm among those whose advice was sought and given at an early stage of the project, but I was not involved in the film's making nor have any stake in it.) Like the book on which it's based, it's a film about risk, and the relationship to risk, individual and collective, personal and political. And it raises the deeply discomforting yet urgent question, as does Malm's book, of what kinds and degrees of risk may be necessary if any of us are serious about bringing the radical break with business-as-usual that's now required—serious, that is, as participants and not just chin-stroking, disinterested observers from the gallery. (There is no gallery in the climate catastrophe.) And yet for the most part the respectable left, and the "climate left" in particular—as it goes through the same-old placid motions of politics-and-activism-as-usual—somehow manages to avoid this very question, even at this late hour.

What could possibly be at the root of this avoidance? It's almost as if a specter haunts the climate left: the specter of revolution, past and future.

2.

To be fair, there are still some on the left who take revolution seriously—at least on a historical, theoretical, and/or aesthetic level—but they tend to haunt only the ivory tower. One thinks of Enzo Traverso's *Revolution: An Intellectual History* (2021) as a recent example of such seriousness. But overall, there's broad agreement that nothing like a mass revolutionary-left movement exists today, other than in the imagination. "The Left seems," Traverso writes in that volume, "to have completely deserted the terrain on which it had, over the last century, accumulated considerable experience and recorded numerous successes: the armed revolution."

Whether armed or not, violent or not, the point is that revolution is approached seriously now only as history, as collective memory and mourning of the heroically vanquished and tragically betrayed. (Traverso explored this phenomenon in his 2016 book, *Left-Wing Melancholia: Marxism, History, and Memory*.) And, most often, as cautionary tale. "The tragedy of revolutions," Traverso writes in *Revolution*, "lies in the fatal metamorphosis that drives them from liberation to the struggle for survival, and finally to the edification of a new oppressive rule; from emancipating violence to coercive violence."

Of course much depends on what one actually means by "revolution." Traverso means "a sudden—and almost always violent—interruption of the historical continuum . . . a break of the social and political order," which sounds about right to me. And on what one means by "seriously."

China Miéville, the acclaimed British novelist and nonfiction writer, wants to revive an explicitly Marxist revolutionary politics, updated for our century. His most recent books, *October: The Story of the Russian Revolution* (2017) and *A Spectre, Haunting* (2022), present the revolution of October 1917 and Marx and Engels's *Communist Manifesto*, respectively, not only as relevant to the present moment but as containing urgent insights and lessons, both positive and negative. Though historical, his project in these books is addressed directly to us, his contemporaries, as political actors, agents of history, potential revolutionary subjects. This is an invigorating and even awe-inspiring act to behold, not least for the way Miéville stares down the reflexive hackles of inveterate cynics. *Fuck the cynics*, Miéville implies. The *Manifesto*'s authors, he reminds us, were "thunderously uncynical," and Miéville, too, is in earnest. He wants us to take revolution seriously not only as intellectual and political history but as living, breathing political practice in the present tense.

Accordingly, Miéville's *A Spectre, Haunting* is both a reintroduction of the *Manifesto* (drawing on the vast literature surrounding it) for a new generation of Marx-curious readers and a defense of revolutionary-left politics against the critics and skeptics, all along the ideological watchtower, who reject any such politics out of hand. "The strongest weapon against revolution, or any hankering for it," he reminds his readers, is "that capitalist-realist common sense that it's impossible, even laughable, to struggle or hope for change. . . . a deliberate ruling-class propaganda strategy to discourage any belief in any such possibility."

But Miéville has no desire to prettify the left's revolutionary history or engage in apologetics—quite the opposite. Nondogmatic, full of caveats, and above all, ethically conscious, he engages the text of the *Manifesto*, its background, and its legacy—much of it brutal and indefensible—in order to preserve or salvage what remains inspiring and useful. To do so requires the readiness to break with Marxist doctrine, to see the past and present without ideological blinders (which is not to say without ideology). In his moving epilogue to *October*, Miéville writes, "We know where this is going:

purges, gulags, starvation, mass murder." But perfect hindsight, he suggests, can breed illusions of inevitability. "Did October lead inexorably to Stalin?" he asks. "It is an old question, but one still very much alive. Is the gulag the telos of 1917?" Miéville would have us resist any such interpretations as the sirens of historical necessity and fatalism. "October is still ground zero for arguments about fundamental, radical social change," he writes. "Its degradation was not a given, was not written in any stars."

What kind of revolution, then, is Miéville hankering for (all caveats and disclaimers duly acknowledged)? Again taking his cue from the *Manifesto* and its authors, he is clearly not advocating a *mere* "political revolution," that which topples a government—even a political system—and replaces it while leaving the underlying social order intact. Nevertheless, Miéville wants a revolutionary left that allows for any number of models, including the possibility of *peaceful* revolution—which, he notes, Marx and Engels themselves did not rule out. What he wants to avoid is "a strain of showboating machismo within the Left" that dismisses anything less than the model of October 1917 "as effete perfidy." Still, he notes, that kind of toxic "border-guarding" no doubt arises in part from "the fact that 'revolutionary' is an easy word to throw around and domesticate." ("They're gonna call us revolutionaries.")

It's clarifying, therefore, when Miéville spells out, in the *Manifesto*'s terms, what he identifies as the three key elements of a Marxist social revolution "worthy of the name." First, he writes, "its aim is rupture. Its point isn't merely amelioration, but the overthrow of the existing order." Second, he tells us, "this is a project with enemies. . . . To the ruling class *as a class*, this is an existential threat, to be fought by any means available. And their counterrevolutionary project might win." The all-important third point, then, is that revolutionists "cannot shy away from the necessity of struggle."

Struggle, rupture, overthrow; but not, necessarily, *by any means.* Miéville is no crude nihilist. He has a genuine concern for the moral-ethical basis of social revolution itself, even as found in the *Manifesto*, despite its authors' claims to have thrown off all bourgeois morality. "The relationship between coercion, force, and violence is crucial here," Miéville writes. "Depending on how much social weight a movement has, how strategically it deploys it, actual *violence*, in no way a good in itself, can be minimized." Indeed, on this crucial question, Miéville goes on to argue that Marx and Engels's judgment of capitalist exploitation and oppression was itself an inherently moral one—as was their vision of the communist alternative. Marx and Engels, he notes, "hold 'so-called civilization' to be itself a barbarous and violent system." It follows, then, Miéville writes: "This is not to be relaxed about violence on any side, but to contest the image of revolution as an irruption of violence into a peaceable system. It's to accept, rather, the necessity of violence against violence, to fight for the end of the mass death and social violence which underpins capitalism, surrounds us, at a greater scale today even than it did the *Manifesto*'s authors."

§

Mass death and social violence at a greater scale today. And so we're back to where we started: a global ecological and social catastrophe driven by "fossil capital" and the demands of untrammeled production and profit—and the effort to stop it somewhere short of total destruction (a civilization-ending scenario that, never mind what you may have heard, is still very much on the table).

To his credit, Miéville addresses the planetary crisis head-on in *A Spectre, Haunting*, but the discussion arrives, as it were, too little and too late, in a brief section sandwiched into the final chapter.

Like so many of his peers among left intellectuals, Miéville is slow to come around to the climate catastrophe. If he took it as seriously as called for, it would frame the whole book; treating it as an afterthought won't do any longer. Climate catastrophe threatens the material conditions on which the whole socialist project rests.

Miéville, as a founding member of the Salvage Collective, knows this well, of course, and it goes to the heart of his response to the crisis:

> To read the *Manifesto* today, is to have to acknowledge that after centuries of exploitation and planetary degradation, the rupture is more urgent than ever—and is unlikely to be into a realm of freedom and plenty, but of necessary slow *repair*.
>
> There is a world to win: won, it must be fixed. This is "ruin communism," or "salvage communism." As part of such project, naïve dreams of profligacy have to be set aside.

Won, it must be fixed. I wish this were convincing. But the problem with Miéville's formulation, and it's not an uncommon one, is the premise that we still have time to "win" the world—on Marxist terms, no less—before we begin to "fix" it (first and foremost by ending the use of fossil fuels). According to climate science, we barely have time to stop the hemorrhaging.

To be sure, Miéville and his Salvage colleagues are perfectly aware of this inherent tension or contradiction. The collective's manifesto, *The Tragedy of the Worker: Towards the Proletarocene* (2021), opens with the sober question—having just quoted Marx and Engels's timeless exhortation to workers, "You have a world to win"—"What if the world is already lost?" It's a question and a tension that's never quite resolved. In the Salvage manifesto's final pages, having led us through a nuanced reimagining of revolutionary Marxism for the age of climate catastrophe, the authors (Miéville, Jamie Allinson, Richard Seymour, and Rosie Warren) conclude:

> In the era of Marx and Engels, and in the long century after, communists dreamed of liberating humanity and enjoying a world of plenty, sharing in abundance. . . . From our benighted vantage point, the birth, growth and exploitation of the working class has been inextricable from biocide and catastrophe. That is to say, global proletarianization and ecological disaster have been products of the same process. The earth the wretched would—will—inherit, will be in need of an assiduous program of restoration. . . . But to have the slightest chance of reaching such a moment, we must strive precisely for a class unbalancing of the earth. . . . the only path to an Anthropocene of a liberated and self-transformed Anthropos runs through the destruction of the Capitalocene, the Proletarocene dawn.

If you have anything like the soul of a leftist, you have to admire the brave words. And yet here again, the "wretched" are envisioned inheriting—winning—the earth before the repair can begin. This may be what Marxist logic requires, but it would seem to reverse the actual, necessary sequence at this emergency juncture of human and planetary history. Before there can be a socialist (not to mention democratic) program of restoration, there must be a livable and salvageable planet on which to organize it—on which stable human societies and something recognizable as a polity can exist—and that in turn requires the urgent, *near*-term (as in, needed-it-yesterday) political means, the mass-movement forces, to defeat the global carbon-industrial regime that's driving the breakdown.

It's an admirable thing to keep the revolutionary flame alive and to make the bold claim that "another world is possible," that the revolution this time may succeed without betraying its principles and devouring its own. It's another thing entirely when you slam up against the hard material limits of actual geophysical conditions—and *time*. Revolutionary Marxism was never meant to operate on a deadline. But today, if you insist that the social revolution, rather than something like the mere bourgeois political variety, must come first—if you must first bring about the Proletarocene dawn—then it is all but certain that there *won't be a world* to win, nothing left to salvage. The world will already be lost.

§

Andreas Malm, whose *Fossil Capital* (2016) excavated the economic roots of climate catastrophe in the beginnings of coal power, is a Marxist intellectual and agitator who not only grasps this grim truth about our situation but says it out loud—even writes entire books about it. In *Corona, Climate, Chronic Emergency: War Communism in the Twenty-First Century* (2020)—which preceded *How to Blow Up a Pipeline* by just a few months in the midst of the pandemic's first year—Malm lays out the case for strong medicine, what he calls "ecological Leninism," to stem the planetary catastrophe. He argues that only centralized state power—"nationalization of all private companies extracting and processing and distributing fossil fuels," along with "comprehensive, airtight planning"—can accomplish what is required in this emergency situation. "Everybody knows this," Malm writes. "Few say it." And so, speed being paramount ("Delay is fatal," as Lenin said), Malm's ecological Leninism "leaps at any opportunity to wrest the state in this direction, break with business-as-usual as sharply as required and subject the regions of the economy working towards catastrophe to direct public control."

But Malm goes further, wisely or not, suggesting that even something like "war communism" may be necessary, invoking the nascent Bolshevik regime's desperate and brutal measures during its struggle to survive the Russian Civil War. Malm, of course, is far from the first to call for something resembling "wartime mobilization" to address the climate emergency, but the term "war communism," he admits, "tends to leave an acid taste. Rightly so." (His use of it, he's quick to add, "is not to suggest that we should have summary executions, send food detachments into the countryside or militarize labor, just as no one who looks at World War II as a model for climate mobilization wants to drop another atomic bomb on Hiroshima.") What Malm is calling for here is not ruthless, unrestrained state power, but an emergency power that's democratically and ethically grounded. He is quite ready to throw out those parts of the Marxist-Leninist playbook that are "ripe (or overripe) for their own obituaries."

Not least among those is the doctrine that prescribes first demolishing the capitalist state and replacing it with a socialist one. The capitalist state is all we have in the near term—and with climate, the near term is what matters. "No workers' state based on soviets will be miraculously born in the night," Malm writes. "Waiting for it would be both delusional and criminal."

What's more, as Malm is well aware, given the current state of our politics there is no reason to assume that any revolutionary rupture will come from the left or result in a left-wing government; if anything, there's more reason to fear a neofascist takeover than any sort of totalitarian left. Malm has explored the intersection of climate and the fascist threat in depth, in his 2021 book with the

Zetkin Collective, *White Skin, Black Fuel: On the Danger of Fossil Fascism.* It's possible that from now on, any viable left will have to resemble a Popular Front antifascist coalition: the fight against fascism and the fight against fossil capital being inseparable.

But Malm makes clear that his ecological Leninism is a conceptual framework, a set of principles, not marching orders. Nor does it imply, he goes on, "that there are any actual Leninist formations capable of seizing power and implementing the correct measures." To the contrary, "The crisis is the absence—the complete, gaping absence—of any leadership." And so the "dreary bourgeois state" will have to be forced, more or less as it now exists, through popular uprising and a diversity of tactics (including "mass sabotage"), to save itself. Then, at least, a reborn revolutionary left may live to fight another day.

However unlikely to be realized Malm's vision may be, and he knows that it appears very unlikely, "those elements of the climate movement and the left that pretend that none of this needs to happen . . . are not being honest," he writes. This rings true. Somebody had to say it.

"Every concrete measure proposed here," Malm concludes, "may well be brushed aside as utopian. They are exactly as utopian as survival."

3·

In the summer of 2013, while on assignment for *The Nation*, I found myself in deep East Texas sitting face-to-face with one of the young organizers of Tar Sands Blockade—the radical grassroots climate-justice campaign drawing energy and recruits from the Occupy movement—engaged for more than a year in sustained nonviolent direct action to stop construction of the Keystone XL pipeline's notorious southern leg from Oklahoma to refineries in

Houston and Port Arthur.

Operating from a clandestine camp outside of Nacogdoches—and, it was later revealed, under surveillance by the FBI's Houston office—the campaign demonstrated a willingness to take serious risks, both legal and physical, and helped galvanize the growing climate-justice movement in North America and Europe. (I told this story at some length in *The Nation* and in *What We're Fighting For Now Is Each Other.*) The question that summer was how the campaign could escalate its tactics beyond the spectacular lockdowns and aerial tree-sit blockades that had made national headlines. "The industry has shown every intention of escalating the climate crisis beyond certain tipping points," the organizer told me. "We need to ask ourselves, 'What does escalation look like? What could possibly be too escalated?'"

That question still haunts.

In *How to Blow Up a Pipeline*, Malm argues that capitalism's sanctification of private property "will cost us the earth," and he goes on to methodically dismantle the social movement doctrine of "strategic nonviolence"—which has long prohibited destruction of property—while remaining resolutely opposed to violence directed against people. Malm is no terrorist. But his frustration with movement orthodoxy is palpable as he inveighs against what he calls "the demise of revolutionary politics," which, he observes, "barely exists any longer as a living praxis":

> From the years 1789 to those around 1989, revolutionary politics maintained actuality and dynamic potentiality, but since the 1980s it has been defamed, antiquated, unlearned and turned unreal. . . . This is the impasse in which the climate movement finds itself: the historical victory of capital and the ruination of the planet are one

and the same thing. To break out of it, we have to learn how to fight all over again.

Malm's book generated a wide and largely unsatisfying debate within the climate movement and the broader left, and it was dismissed, unsurprisingly, by a lot of very serious people (including activists and policy advocates) as fringe and dangerous. This was a very serious mistake. Nothing could be more dangerous at this moment in human history than an unfounded faith in politics-and-activism as usual, and an unwillingness to take necessary, calculated risks.

Around the time *How to Blow Up a Pipeline* was belatedly discovered by the mainstream press, I was asked by a reporter for a major newspaper, off the record, just how far I'd be willing to go as an activist in the struggle against the fossil-fuel industry and its political backers. I told him, speaking as one who has supported and engaged in escalated nonviolent direct action for more than a decade, that I honestly didn't know. (And if I did know, I probably wouldn't tell a reporter, on or off the record.) Truth is, I still don't. But it's a good question—the same one that's haunted me since 2013—and not only for a climate activist. It's a question that anyone involved in left politics should be asking themselves now.

The answer no doubt depends upon how you understand the present moment—whether you've really taken on board, not only rationally but viscerally, based on the prevailing scientific and political realities, just how desperate the human situation on this planet really is, especially for the vast majority of the world's population who have done little or nothing to cause the catastrophe. After thirty-plus years of failure on climate policy by the Global North, with global greenhouse emissions still at record levels, surely any informed and decent person living in one of the world's most historically culpable countries will be moved to ask what can and must be done to at least reduce the suffering and salvage a livable future—one with the possibility of social and economic justice.

Chances are, though, even if you identify as a socialist of some sort, the option of engaging in a revolutionary-left movement won't cross your mind. Maybe you'd prefer, if you can afford it, to go shopping instead: buy an EV, an electric heat pump, some solar panels for your roof. Too bourgeois? Then perhaps switch to a plant-based diet; attend a protest; canvass for a political candidate; maybe even get arrested—and post about all of it on social media. All good and worthwhile things. But actually try to help bring about the urgent and necessary radical break with the political and economic system that's driving the destruction? In a country crawling with heavily armed right-wing militants and a militarized police/surveillance state itching to use its latest toys? *What sort of fool do you think I am?*

At this point, one might reasonably ask: If any serious revolutionary-left politics has been all but dead for at least a generation or two, and if there's no sign on the horizon of a movement capable of taking power and forcing the radical shift required—if even "mere" Bernie Sanders–style political revolution appears far-fetched at present—what is the point of talking about any of this? Why bother?

In fact, one might just as well ask what the point is, at this late hour, of talking about *any* alternative political, social, or ecological vision—of *any* hope that a better world, even a salvaged one, is still possible—without taking seriously the urgent necessity of a *radical rupture*. For the climate movement and the broader left to settle for anything less than "mere" political revolution—to resign ourselves to head-in-sand incrementalism while dreaming of an abundant green socialism—is to settle for a global ecocide amounting to genocide for large parts of humanity.

If this is the case, then the task for those of us who refuse to settle, and who choose to engage, is to urgently shift our social movements, in broad solidarity and coalition, toward *the making or remaking of a revolutionary left politics.* This means building a "movement of movements," as many of us have insisted for years, that's committed to rupture, ready to shut things down, to hasten the crisis global capitalism pretends it can avoid, and to use our democratic power effectively.

This, in turn, means building a movement culture of risk-taking, both personal and collective; of sacrifice, when necessary; and of resolve, once committed, to stay in the fight.

And the risks are, indeed, enormous. (Just ask Jessica Reznicek and Ruby Montoya, climate-justice activists who were sentenced to eight and six years in prison, respectively, for their nonviolent sabotage of the Dakota Access Pipeline in 2016.) But the alternative—climate breakdown plus fascism, eco-/genocide, in short, barbarism—is intolerable. Business, politics, and activism as usual are already catastrophic. Continuing on the current path is the greatest risk of all. There are, in fact, no safe options.

As I'm sure Malm would admit, it's possible that literally blowing up pipelines will not turn out to be the wisest of tactics, for reasons that he and I discussed in our December 2020 interview, from political blowback to security-state repression. What we can say, as any seasoned movement strategist knows, is that a revolutionary act, no matter how spectacular, does not make a revolutionary movement. Revolutionary tactics do not, of themselves, amount to a revolutionary politics. Only movements are capable of revolution.

But I'm with Malm in the assessment that the willingness to take large risks—including the willingness to break things, in particular the things that are breaking the very biosphere—would seem a minimum requirement for any revolutionary-left movement worthy of the name. That is, any movement that takes seriously not only human survival but human solidarity—that most utopian of ends—for which many in history, let us never forget, have risked and given everything. And for which some of us, it may yet be discovered, still will.

TEN

The Desperate of the Earth

Frantz Fanon and the Search for Human Solidarity

SEPTEMBER 2024

There is a famous line in The Wretched of the Earth *where Frantz Fanon writes of violence as a 'cleansing force.' It frees the native 'from his despair and inaction; it makes him fearless and restores his self-respect.' Few processes produce as much despair as global heating. Imagine that, someday, the reservoirs of that emotion built up around the world—in the Global South in particular—find their outlets. There has been a time for a Gandhian climate movement; perhaps there might come time for a Fanonian one.*
—Andreas Malm, *How to Blow Up a Pipeline* (2021)

We believe that in the cases presented here the triggering factor is principally the bloody, pitiless atmosphere, the generalization of inhuman practices. . . . it is the war, this colonial war that very often takes on the aspect of a genuine genocide. . .
—Frantz Fanon, "Colonial War and Mental Disorders,"
    The Wretched of the Earth (1961)

1.

This is no simple morality tale. It's not a Sunday school lesson for the choir—unless yours is the sort of Sunday school (or political movement) that respects life, in all of its actuality and contradiction, and not the comforts of dogma.

On June 8, 2024, an image spread across Israeli media, and then the world's, of a weeping father reunited with his young-adult daughter—abducted by Hamas on October 7, 2023—clutching her in his arms like life itself, as though she had been raised from the dead. The image possesses a kind of mythical, even biblical, timelessness and power. If one feels no stirring of sympathy for this father and child, then it is possible that some part of one's humanity has gone missing.

And yet that image holds only a partial, and a sanitized, truth. Among the truths not shown are the corpses of some 274 Palestinians, mainly civilians—many of them children—ruthlessly bombarded by the Israeli military in its operation to free that young woman and three other Israeli hostages held in the Nuseirat refugee camp in central Gaza, where displaced families fleeing Israel's genocidal campaign had taken shelter. Few incidents of the war to that point revealed quite so clearly what value the far-right Zionist regime places on innocent Palestinian lives—namely, zero. Or, rather, a negative value—after all, "there are no innocent Palestinians," we've been told since October 7. Israel's indiscriminate bombing campaign against Gaza's dense urban population—which military experts have called "unprecedented" in its concentrated intensity—had killed more than thirty-seven thousand Palestinians as of that June (and at least forty-six thousand by year's end), most of them civilians, the majority women and children. For Israel's leaders, the Jewish state's right of "self-defense" means that Palestinians, as many of them as possible, must die. "We are fighting human animals and we are acting accordingly," said Israeli defense minister Yoav Gallant, announcing a "complete siege"—"no electricity, no food, no fuel, everything is closed"—and total war against Gaza's population of 2.2 million trapped and dehumanized human beings.

Such statements of intent are among the evidence compelling the UN's International Court of Justice to demand that Israel cease operations leading to a "plausible" genocide in Gaza—and the International Criminal Court in The Hague to request warrants for Gallant and Israeli prime minister Benjamin Netanyahu on charges of war crimes and crimes against humanity, supported by the investigative report of a special UN commission.

But not only warrants for Israel's leaders. The ICC and UN commission have stated that Hamas, too, committed war crimes and crimes against humanity in its October 7 operation, Toufan al-Aqsa (Al-Aqsa Flood).

This is not the false "objectivity" of journalistic both-sides-ism; it's mere honesty. If one is going to justify or condone Hamas's actions on October 7, as some on the left have been ready to do, then surely one must look squarely at what was done, what one is actually justifying. According to the UN commission, Hamas fighters that day went house to house, slaughtering at least eight hundred Israeli civilians—women, children, entire families. Some 250 people were taken hostage, including children and the elderly. (And the victims were not only Israelis but also civilians of other nationalities, including migrant workers and students from Asia and Africa.) The commission found evidence of rape and sexual violence committed by Hamas fighters, though it remains unclear to what extent, if any, this was policy (Hamas leadership denies all such accusations). Supposing one argues that the more than three hundred Israeli military and security personnel killed in the raid

were legitimate targets, not of terrorism but of an armed struggle for national liberation (a not-unreasonable position), one still
must account for the methodical massacre of those hundreds of
noncombatants and, most of all, the innocent children. How is this
not similar—in execution if not scale—to the genocidal "collective punishment" of a specific ethnic and/or national population
for which Israel must be held accountable in Gaza? How can there
be any serious discussion of Israel's crimes against humanity if the
crimes of Hamas are ignored at one's convenience?

The charge of genocide, considered the worst of crimes against
humanity, requires, to begin with, the acknowledgment of the
equal humanity of all. My body fills with grief for all the dead and
captive Israeli Jews and their families—no less, and no more, than
for the dead, maimed, starved, and displaced Palestinians of Gaza.
How could it not, if I am to call myself a human being?

In case you're wondering, I have personally stood, marched,
and protested in solidarity with Palestinian lives—offered my tangible support to student protesters (many of them young Jews) in
Boston and Cambridge, Massachusetts—and joined the call for
Palestinian freedom "from the river to the sea" (a phrase, by the
way, that is also a historic rallying cry of right-wing Zionism). *Not*
for the violent destruction of Israel or the death of Jews. The Zionist apartheid state as currently constituted may well have no right
to exist—but the people of Israel, and Jews everywhere, most certainly do. This should go without saying, but here in the belly of
empire, the United States of America—where practically any call
for Palestinian freedom is equated with genocidal antisemitism—it
must be said anyway. I will never be in solidarity with Hamas and
those like them, not as long as they massacre defenseless Jewish
families, murder children in cold blood, and act with reckless—or
worse, strategic, premeditated—disregard for the lives and welfare

of their fellow Palestinians, bringing certain death and destruction down upon them. (I am not alone in this, of course; I join plenty of Palestinians and their allies in rejecting Hamas.) It has been noted, by Tareq Baconi and others, that Hamas years ago made a strategic shift away from the "martyrdom operations" (suicide bombings) of the Second Intifada. And yet, Toufan al-Aqsa has made involuntary "martyrs" of tens of thousands of Palestinian civilians. If you are a Palestinian mother or child, your life apparently means little or nothing to the leaders of Hamas—you are a mere instrument, an expendable body, a useful corpse, an abstract datum in the cold, nihilistic calculus of ends and means.

And yet for all of this, there is another basic truth that must be faced: the "resistance" that Hamas represents and the actions of October 7, 2023, were born of nothing less than desperation—after fifteen years under the Israeli blockade of Gaza, more than a half century of military occupation and expansionist settler violence in the West Bank, and three quarters of a century since the Nakba. The history of anticolonial resistance and revolution is, first and foremost, not that of ideology; it is a history of the desperate. For it is the desperate, those with little or nothing to lose—the true "wretched of the earth," as the old internationalist anthem says— who will risk everything, and do anything, to escape their intolerable situation.

§

A decade ago, it might have been presumptuous or simply tone deaf, especially for a writer in my privileged position, to leap from the dire situation of the Palestinian people to the seemingly distant, as if abstract, injustices of climate and ecological crisis. Today, not so much. The onslaught of global warming and ecocide amounting to genocide across much of the postcolonial and neocolonized Global South is now widely understood to be underway (it was underway ten years ago, too). And in a place as exposed as Palestine to the inhuman ravages of unsurvivable heat, drought, and desertification—amplified and compounded by the inhuman ravages of colonialist apartheid and genocidal war—the two catastrophes, Nakba and climate, converge. If you're looking for a single spot on the planet where the twenty-first-century conditions of the Global South begin, you won't find a better one than Israel's wall of separation—on one side a prosperous, militarized, high-tech capitalist society, on the other a seething population of refugees. The long Palestinian struggle for survival—rooted in the historic and, yes, holy land on either side of that wall—takes on new meaning as the land itself becomes uninhabitable. For both populations.

Gaza is already all but uninhabitable—Israel's war and its American-made, American-blessed bombs have seen to that.

Indeed, there is perhaps no place on earth where the atrocities of fossil-capitalist imperialism, tribalistic ethnoreligious nationalisms, and oncoming climate catastrophe intersect as plainly and brutally as in Gaza and the whole of Israel–Palestine (unless it were Darfur, or Syria, or Myanmar, or Xinjiang—or the US southern border). It's hard to think of a clearer test of the global climate-justice movement, and in fact many in the movement have made common cause with Palestine. As I write this, hundreds of young climate-justice and pro-Palestinian activists are facing arrest and police repression on the public plaza in front of Citibank's global headquarters in lower Manhattan, demanding an end to the bank's funding of the Israeli military and its role among the top financiers of catastrophic fossil-fuel expansion.

But there's more to this test than simply drawing these obvious connections. At stake is no less than the very nature of the struggle for humanity's future—the nature of the climate-justice movement and of the left itself—in the era of catastrophic warming. Because nowhere does the abyss of nihilism and despair open wider, nowhere is any kind of illumination, as Hannah Arendt might say—or any genuine human solidarity—harder to find, or more desperately needed.

And this is why we need not only Arendt and the other humanist thinkers discussed in this book—but also, perhaps surprisingly, the anticolonial revolutionary Frantz Fanon. The actual, complicated, contradictory Fanon.

2.

Among the inspirations and models for the armed Palestinian struggle was Algeria's Front de Libération Nationale, the FLN, which led the Algerian war of independence from France in which Fanon was deeply involved. As Alistair Horne tells it in *A Savage War of Peace: Algeria 1954–1962*, by the summer of 1955, less than a year into its anticolonial revolution, the FLN's armed struggle was running out of steam, in danger of stalling entirely under brutal French military repression.

Only one of the FLN's regional sectors, Wilaya 2, centered around Constantine in Algeria's northeast, had sufficient forces to mount a potentially game-changing operation. "In a mood almost of desperation," Horne writes, regional commanders Youssef Zighout and Lakhdar Ben Tobbal "convened a council of war at the end of June to launch, for the first time, a policy of total war on all French civilians, regardless of age and sex." In justifying the shift, Horne tells us,

> Zighout declared: "To colonialism's policy of *collective repression* . . . we must reply with collective reprisals against the Europeans, military and civil, who are all united behind

the crimes committed upon our people. For them, no pity, no quarter!" Simultaneously with military action by cadres of the F.L.N., a true "people's revolt" was to be unleashed in the Constantine region, in which "the largest possible number of Algerians, even hastily armed with only sticks, pitchforks, axes, sickles and knives," was to be involved.

The attacks came on August 20 and focused on the coastal town of Philippeville and the surrounding area. Among the first to be killed, in Constantine, was the nephew of the Algerian moderate nationalist leader Ferhat Abbas, executed for his past criticism of the FLN.

Horne goes on to describe the ensuing violence in unsparing detail. In Phillipeville, Algerian men and women "swarmed into the streets," he writes. "Grenades were thrown indiscriminately into cafés, passing European motorists dragged from their vehicles and slashed to death with knives or even razors." At El-Halia, a mining town near Philippeville where Europeans and Algerian Muslims had lived side by side for years ("amicably enough," according to Horne), attackers went house to house slaughtering whole *pied noir* (French settler) families. "In houses literally awash with blood, European mothers were found with their throats slit and their bellies slashed open by billhooks. Children had suffered the same fate, and infants in arms had had their brains dashed out against the wall. . . . Men returning home from the mine had been ambushed in their cars and hacked to pieces." At Ain-Abid, Horne tells us, where another *pied noir* family was murdered, including a seventy-three-year-old grandmother and an eleven-year-old girl and her father (his limbs hacked off in his bed), the mother "had been disemboweled, her five-day-old baby slashed to death and replaced in her opened womb." Such sickening scenes, Horne goes on to say, must be described if one is to understand how the Philippeville massacre changed the course of the Algerian war.

As in the aftermath of the bloody Sétif uprising in May 1945 (in which 103 Europeans were killed and many thousands of Algerian civilians slaughtered in retaliation), the FLN fully expected French reprisals to be disproportionate in the extreme. Nevertheless, Horne writes, "Zighout and Ben Tobbal accepted that the [Algerian civilian] losses would be severe." Indeed, such was the strategy: the French response would lead to new popular support of the FLN's war effort. Horne is equally unsparing in his descriptions of the French atrocities. He captures the scene at Philippeville in the words of a French paratrooper whose regiment was among the first to arrive. Upon encountering militants ("rebels") mixed in with civilians, the French soldier recalls:

> We opened fire into the thick of them, at random. Then as we moved on and found more [European] bodies, our company commanders finally gave us the order to shoot down every Arab we met. You should have seen the result. . . . For two hours all we heard was automatic rifles spitting fire into the crowd. . . . At midday, fresh orders: take prisoners. That complicated everything. It was easy when it was merely a matter of killing. . . . At six o'clock next morning, all the LMGs and machine guns were lined up in front of the crowd of prisoners, who immediately began to yell. But we opened fire; ten minutes later, it was practically over. There were so many of them that they had to be buried with bulldozers.

French authorities said seventy-one European settlers were killed on August 20, and 1,273 "insurgents." But the number of

Algerian civilians slaughtered by the army and *pied noir* vigilantes was almost certainly much higher. Horne notes that the FLN, "giving names and addresses," put the number at twelve thousand.

By the war's end in 1962, with the achievement of independence, an estimated three hundred thousand to one million Algerians were dead, the vast majority of them civilians, tens of thousands of them at the hands of the FLN and rival factions in what amounted to near civil war—and among them countless innocent bystanders, victims of internal purges and terrorist bombs. The French torture of Algerian prisoners became routine. French military losses included more than seventeen thousand killed and sixty-five thousand wounded or missing. More than three thousand *pied noir* civilians died, many in terrorist attacks and bombings by the FLN, others in terrorist bombings by right-wing settler militia groups in the war's final year. At independence, well over a million *pied noir* fled their homes for France, where they were alien and unwanted.

§

Albert Camus, a third-generation *pied noir* from a *petit blanc* (poor white) family, may have called Algeria his true home, but no writer of world renown is more closely associated with the Algerian war of independence than the radical psychiatrist from Martinique, Frantz Fanon, whose classic treatise *The Wretched of the Earth* (*Les damnés de la terre*, published in late 1961, just before his early death from leukemia) catapulted him posthumously into the pantheon of Third World revolutionary thinkers. And not merely associated; Fanon was deeply embedded with the FLN, a member of the editorial board of its Tunis-based newspaper, *El Moudjahid*, and one of its chief propagandists to the outside world.

The famous/infamous opening chapter of *The Wretched of the Earth*, "On Violence," which so enraptured Jean-Paul Sartre—upon whom Fanon prevailed to write the book's controversial introduction—has long been cited by admirers and detractors for its bracing, cold-blooded justification of anticolonial violence. (Hannah Arendt, in her 1969 essay "On Violence," partly a response to Fanon's popularity with New Left radicals, remarked that Sartre "in his glorification of violence" went "farther than Fanon himself" and that if Sartre's faith in a violence "that heals" were valid, "revenge would be the cure-all for most of our ills.") Fanon's recent biographer Adam Shatz, in *The Rebel's Clinic: The Revolutionary Lives of Frantz Fanon* (2024), notes that some readers "have expressed horror at Fanon's defense of violence, accusing him of being an apologist for terrorism." It's not hard to see why, given his role with the FLN and his often-chilling language ("For the colonized, life can only materialize from the rotting cadaver of the colonist"). But as Shatz goes on to argue, Fanon's writing on the subject of violence often lends itself to misreading and even caricature.

In fact there's far more to Fanon than his radical-chic image as prophet of violent anticolonial revolution—not least his antiracist humanism and antiracialist understanding of identity. First, though, one must get past the simplistic and reductive hero worship. This broader, more complicated, and more profound Fanon is the one we need in our own moment. And in order to salvage Fanon the humanist, we have to contend with what he actually said about violence.

"At the individual level, violence is a cleansing force," Fanon writes (as translated by Richard Philcox in the standard Grove Press edition, reissued in 2021), in what is perhaps the most quoted passage from the opening chapter of *The Wretched of the Earth*. "It rids the colonized of their inferiority complex, of their passive and despairing attitude. It emboldens them and restores their self-confidence." Shatz points out that the most provocative phrase here, "violence is a cleansing force"—often repeated in sound-bite form by Fanon's Western followers—is a "somewhat misleading" translation from the French. Fanon's original phrase—*la violence désintoxique*—could be literally rendered, as Shatz has it, "violence is dis-intoxicating." In other words, Fanon presents the outbreak of anticolonial violence not as cleansing or purifying, much less redemptive, as some would have it, but more like a sobering cold shower, as if to jolt the colonized out of their stupor.

But there's more to the misreading than one phrase. In the pages preceding that unfortunately translated money quote, Fanon is concerned not so much to celebrate or promote the raging violence unleashed at the outset of anticolonial revolution but rather, as if with the clinical eye of the psychiatrist, to describe and analyze it in order to understand and explain its significance. "The violence of the colonial regime and the counterviolence of the colonized balance each other and respond to each other in an extraordinary reciprocal homogeneity," Fanon writes. A "point of no return," he observes, "was reached in Algeria in 1955 with the 12,000 victims of Philippeville. . . . To the expression: 'All natives are the same,' the colonized reply: 'All colonists are the same.' . . . On the logical plane, the Manichaeanism of the colonist produces a Manichaeanism of the colonized."

Granted, if all you've read of *The Wretched of the Earth* is that opening chapter, and if you ignore Fanon's clinical-analytical approach, then you might indeed get the impression of Fanon as cold-blooded apostle of unlimited forms of violence—"any means necessary." Such was the FLN's policy, after all, and he was among its spokespersons. And yet, in subsequent chapters, Fanon injects far more critical and cautionary notes, warning against what he called "pure, total brutality." It's important to quote some of these passages at length, to dispense with the sound bites, see Fanon in full light, and absorb his nuanced cadences. In the second chapter, "Grandeur and Weakness of Spontaneity," Fanon writes:

> Antiracist racism and the determination to defend one's skin, which is characteristic of the colonized's response to colonial oppression, clearly represent sufficient reasons to join the struggle. But one does not sustain a war, one does not endure massive repression or witness the disappearance of one's entire family in order for hatred or racism to triumph. Racism, hatred, resentment, and "the legitimate desire for revenge" alone cannot nurture a war of liberation. These flashes of consciousness which fling the body into a zone of turbulence, which plunge it into a virtually pathological dreamlike state where the sight of the other induces vertigo, where my blood calls for the blood of the other, where my death through mere inertia calls for the death of the other, this passionate outburst in the opening phase, disintegrates if it is left to feed on itself. . . . [D]ay by day, leaders will come to realize that hatred is not an agenda.

For some reason, passages like this one are less often quoted by Fanon enthusiasts. Maybe that's because Fanon, here and in what follows, directly challenges the Manichaean racist worldview he had earlier described (but not endorsed) and argues that the anticolonial movement must move beyond it. "The people," Fanon writes, "who in the early days of the struggle had adopted the primitive Manichaeanism of the colonizer—Black versus White, Arab versus Infidel—realize en route that some blacks can be whiter than the whites."

He continues:

> The idyllic, unreal clarity of the early days is replaced by a
> penumbra which dislocates the consciousness. . . . On their
> arduous path to rationality the people must also learn to give
> up their simplistic perception of the oppressor. . . . Some
> members of the colonialist population prove to be closer,
> infinitely closer, to the nationalist struggle than certain na-
> tive sons. The racial and racist dimension is transcended
> on both sides. Not every black or Muslim is automatically
> given a vote of confidence. One no longer grabs a gun or a
> machete every time a colonist approaches. Consciousness
> stumbles upon partial, finite, and shifting truths.

One has to wonder if there isn't a subtle self-critique contained here. Recall that Fanon had been there in the early days of
the FLN's war—there was no more ardent supporter—but he had
also seen where such revolutionary Manichaeanism had led. Unable
or unwilling to engage in direct criticism of FLN methods, Fanon
seems to have couched his doubts carefully in passages such as these:

> In spite of those within the movement, who sometimes
> are inclined to think that any nuance constitutes a dan-
> ger and threatens popular solidarity, the leadership stands
> by the principles worked out in the national struggle and
> in the universal fight conducted by man for his liberation.
> There is a brutality and contempt for subtleties and indi-
> vidual cases which is typically revolutionary, but there is
> another type of brutality with surprising resemblances to
> the first one which is typically counterrevolutionary, ad-
> venturist, and anarchist. If this pure, total brutality is not

immediately contained it will, without fail, bring down the movement within a few weeks.

As a psychiatrist, Fanon had seen the mental and physical casualties of such brutality, at the psychiatric hospital he ran in Blida, south of Algiers, where he treated both Algerian and French patients, soldiers and civilians. And in the pages of *The Wretched of the Earth*, Fanon builds an argument for a movement that would go beyond the Manichaean brutality of the FLN's tactics—however much in response to equally brutal French repression—and toward something more, as we can see, universal: not just one nation's or people's independence but human liberation, a movement that could transcend race, nationality, religion, culture, even class. It was no less an anticolonialist than Edward Said who wrote, in *Culture and Imperialism* (1993), "Throughout *The Wretched of the Earth* (written in French), Fanon wants somehow to bind the European as well as the native together in a new non-adversarial community of awareness and anti-imperialism."

In other words, what Fanon wanted was a kind of movement, in the case of Algeria—where sub-Saharan Africans were confronted with considerable anti-Black racism—that would welcome Fanon himself, always an outsider, never fully trusted by FLN leaders. Fanon, let's be clear, was a Black-bourgeois-Martinican Frenchman, an enfranchised citizen of the Republic and university-educated intellectual, who had lived a mere two years on Algerian soil before escaping along with the FLN's top leadership to Tunis (with his wife Marie-Josèphe Dublé, a white Frenchwoman, and their child); who spoke impeccable French but not Arabic or Amizagh (the indigenous Berber language); who knew little, and seemed to care even less, about Islam, the foundation of Algerian society; and yet who had the audacity to proclaim himself an Algerian. If that's not some sort of universalism, what is?

§

It was in Fanon's first book, *Black Skin, White Masks* (1952)—prized today for its forward-looking insights into racial identity and colonialism—that he first made his yearning for a radical new humanism, beyond race and nationality, most explicit. Again, it's well worth quoting Fanon at some length, in order to get the full force of the incantatory, even prophetic prose of the book's opening and closing chapters.

In no sense advocating a facile color blindness, Fanon establishes from the outset his determination to "demystify" the racial essentialism in which he sees both the colonized person of color and the European trapped and, in effect, dehumanized. "Running the risk of angering my black brothers, I shall say that a Black is not a man," Fanon writes in his introduction (and, yes, his language is relentlessly gendered). "There is a zone of nonbeing," he goes on, "an extraordinarily sterile and arid region, an incline stripped bare of every essential from which a genuine new departure can emerge." This zone, for the Black person, is a prison, a "veritable hell," Fanon assures us. And yet, continuing in this existential vein, he then upends any expectations of the racial pessimism so common today. "Man is not only the potential for self-consciousness or negation," Fanon writes. "If it be true that consciousness is transcendental, we must also realize that this transcendence is obsessed with the issue of love and understanding. Man is a 'yes' resonating from cosmic harmonies."

There's more Martin than Malcolm in these pages of Fanon's, as if he's heralding the sonorous universalism of MLK, a decade or more before King reached his zenith. "We believe that an individual must endeavor to assume the universalism inherent in the human condition," Fanon states. Of course, like both King and Malcolm X, Fanon was a revolutionary, insisting on social transformation,

not individual awakening, as the only real cure for structurally racist oppression. But he also preached, as they did, that the source
of collective power lies in the power of self-transformation—the
power to "dis-alienate" oneself, as Fanon put it—within each of
us as individuals. And this humanistic emphasis on the person, in
relationship with other persons, leads Fanon to some of his most
powerful affirmations:

> I find myself one day in the world, and I acknowledge
> one right for myself: the right to demand human behavior
> from the other.
>
> And one duty: the duty never to let my decisions re-
> nounce my freedom. . . .
>
> I am not a slave to [the] slavery that dehumanized my
> ancestors. . . .
>
> I, a man of color, want but one thing:
>
> May man never be instrumentalized. May the subjuga-
> tion of man by man—that is to say, of me by another—cease.
> May I be allowed to discover and desire man wherever he
> may be.
>
> The black man is not. No more than the white man.
>
> Both have to move away from the inhuman voices of
> their respective ancestors so that a genuine communica-
> tion can be born. . . .
>
> Superiority? Inferiority?
>
> Why not simply try to touch the other, feel the other,
> discover each other?

Perhaps readers of *The Wretched of the Earth* would do well to
take these prior words of its author to heart.

§

For Fanon, this "genuine communication," discovery of self and other, came to be through his years of clinical psychiatric practice, first in France and then in Algeria and Tunisia. By all accounts, Fanon, though he could be stern and authoritarian with his staff, was a remarkably sensitive and empathetic listener whose openness encouraged his deeply damaged patients to trust him with their harrowing stories of wartime trauma and often severe symptoms of mental illness. This is the Fanon we encounter in the stunning final chapter of *The Wretched of the Earth*, "Colonial War and Mental Disorders," where he offers a series of case histories of Algerian, French, and *pied noir* patients. In the end, we're left with a very different image of Fanon than that of the mythologized apostle of radical violence. Indeed, I would suggest, along with Shatz, that this often-ignored chapter presents a counternarrative and counterbalance to the book's opening chapter, revealing subtle yet unmistakable misgivings, possibly regrets, about the Algerian war's human costs.

There is the case of the thirty-seven-year-old *fellah*, a peasant uninvolved in "politics," who was wounded in a French army massacre of his village and lined up with twenty-nine other men to be shot but miraculously managed to escape. Now afflicted with "random homicidal impulses," attacking patients, nurses, and doctors in the hospital ward, he tells Fanon: "There are some French among us. . . . They're disguised as Arabs. . . . They've all got to be killed. . . . I'll kill them all, every one of them. I'll slit their throats, one after the other, and yours as well. . . . Killing you won't affect me in the slightest. The little ones, the grown-ups, the women, the children, the dogs, the birds, the donkeys . . . nobody will be spared."

There is the nineteen-year-old former student, a fighter in the Armée de Libération Nationale (the armed wing of the FLN), who suffers "major depressive disorder with mood-congruent psychotic features," having disemboweled a *pied noir* woman who reminded him of his mother, shot point-blank by a French soldier. His unit had come looking for the woman's husband, "a notorious colonial," but he wasn't at home. "I kept looking at the woman and thinking of my mother. . . . She threw herself on me screaming: 'Please . . . don't kill me. . . . I've got children.' The next minute she was dead. I'd killed her with my knife." Later, he tells Fanon, "I began to vomit after eating and I slept badly. After that this woman would come every night asking for my blood. And what about my mother's blood?"

There is the twenty-eight-year-old European police officer whose job involved torturing Algerian prisoners and who now suffers acute depression and anxiety, "having difficulty sleeping at night because he kept hearing screams." He tries closing the windows and shutters, though it's summer and stiflingly hot, puts cotton in his ears, turns on the radio, "so as not to hear the nightly din," Fanon writes. "I can tell just which stage the interrogation has reached by the sound of the screams," he says to Fanon. "Now I can hear those screams even at home. Especially the screams of the ones who died at the police headquarters. Doctor, I'm sick of this job. If you can cure me, I'll request a transfer to France. If they refuse, I'll resign."

This is immediately followed by the case of a European police inspector who spends long hours torturing prisoners and has started beating his young children and tying up his wife in "fits of madness" when he gets home. He tells Fanon: "The thing that gets me the most is the torture. Does that mean anything to you? . . . Sometimes I torture for ten hours straight. . . . It wears you out." With no intention of resigning his job, Fanon writes, "he asked me in plain language to help him torture Algerian patriots without having a guilty conscience."

And there is the twenty-one-year-old Frenchwoman, a student, with "alarming" symptoms of anxiety, chest constrictions, and migraines, whose father was a civil servant in charge of a large rural district. She tells Fanon:

> As soon as the troubles broke out, he threw himself like a maniac into a frenzied manhunt for Algerians. . . . every time I went home the screams coming from downstairs kept me awake at night. They were torturing Algerians in the cellar . . . You can't imagine how horrible it is to hear screams like that all through the night. . . . You see I'd lived for a long time in the village. I know almost all the families. I had played with the young Algerians of my age when we were little. . . . Deep down I knew the Algerians were right. If I were Algerian I'd join the resistance movement.

Earlier in the chapter, as Fanon introduces his methodology and his approach in presenting the cases, he explains his belief that the "triggering factor" in all of these disorders "is principally the bloody, pitiless atmosphere, the generalization of inhuman practices." And it is the war itself, he writes, "this colonial war that very often takes on the aspect of a genuine genocide." It's interesting that he doesn't specify the perpetrators and victims of genocide here. But the chapter's most suggestive case—itself an outlier, in that it's a "medical and legal examination" that took place in a prison, not a hospital—subtly subverts our expectations. The case is that of two Algerian schoolboys, ages thirteen and fourteen, who have admitted to murdering a working-class *pied noir* playmate whose father, a mason, is a member of a French militia. Fanon's account is rendered partly in dialogue:

a. The thirteen-year-old:

"We were not angry with him. . . . He was our best friend. . . . One day we decided to kill him because the Europeans want to kill all the Arabs. . . . So we took a knife from home and we killed him."

"But why did you pick on him?"

"Because he used to play with us. Another boy wouldn't have gone up the hill with us."

"But he was a friend of yours?"

"So, why do they want to kill us? His father's in the militia and says we all ought to have our throats slit."

"But [your friend] didn't say anything like that to you?"

"Him? No."

"You know he's dead now."

"Yes. . . ."

"Are you sorry you killed someone?"

"No, because they want to kill us . . . "

b. The fourteen-year-old:

". . . tell me why you killed this boy who was your friend?"

"I'll tell you. . . . Have you heard about the Rivet business?" [a village near Algiers massacred by French militia]

"Yes."

"Two of my family were killed that day. At home they say the French had sworn to kill us all. . . . I wanted to take to the mountains [to join the resistance], but I'm too young. So [the other boy] and I said . . . we would kill a European."

"Why? . . . you are a child and the things that are going on are for grown-ups."

"But they kill children too."

"But that's no reason for killing your friend."

"Well, I killed him. Now you can do what you like."

"Did this friend do anything to you?"

"No. He didn't do anything."

"Well?"

"That's all there is to it."

No reason for killing your friend, Fanon says. Not exactly an endorse-
ment of indiscriminate anticolonial violence or the total war on civilians waged by the FLN.

Another suggestive case is the one Fanon relates at the outset, to introduce the others: that of a former resistance fighter in
an unnamed formerly colonized African country (possibly Tunisia,
where Fanon was living), who had placed a bomb in a café, killing ten people, and is now "afflicted with insomnia together with
anxiety attacks and obsession with suicide around a certain date in
the year" (the date the bombing took place). "This militant," Fanon
tells us, "who never for a moment had thought of recanting, fully
realized the price he had had to pay in his person for national independence. Such borderline cases pose the question of responsibility
in the context of the revolution." And then Fanon adds the most
telling of footnotes, one you're unlikely to see quoted along with
the usual sound bites. It appears that not long after independence,
this militant made friends with several French nationals. "These
men and women welcomed the newly acquired independence,"
Fanon writes, "and unhesitatingly paid tribute to the courage of the
patriots in the national liberation struggle. The militant was then
overcome by a kind of vertigo. He anxiously asked himself whether
among the victims of his bomb there might have been individuals
similar to his new acquaintances."

"In other words," Fanon confesses, "our actions never cease to
haunt us."

§

The contradiction at the heart of *The Wretched of the Earth* and
perhaps of Fanon's life—that between his commitment to armed

anticolonial struggle and the humanistic, even humanitarian, values underlying his psychiatric practice—may finally be irresolvable. Unless, that is, we agree that the armed struggle for liberation, as Fanon saw it, is itself rooted in a kind of radical humanism. To violently throw off colonial oppression, to liberate oneself and others from slavery or any form of dehumanizing totalitarian domination, is an assertion of one's humanity by the only viable means available. Who among us would argue today that the bloody war to end slavery in America, itself fought on universal humanistic grounds, was unjustified? And surely the war to liberate Europe from Hitler, in which Fanon fought and was wounded wearing a Free French uniform, can be viewed as a struggle rooted in humanistic ideals—even if Britain, the United States, and the Soviet Union were also responsible for war crimes and crimes against humanity (unindicted at Nuremberg) in the targeting of civilian populations.

In other words, perhaps it is not violence, per se, that is always and everywhere inhuman; it matters how and why and against whom, and within what limits, liberatory violence is brought to bear. Fanon certainly never wavered on the necessity of armed struggle, but he seems to have harbored serious doubts about the strategic, indiscriminate targeting of civilians, which he saw spiral into genocidal communal warfare (precisely what Camus had warned against in his dead-on-arrival "Plea for a Civilian Truce"). For Fanon, there seems to have been an ethical boundary, rooted in shared humanistic values, the crossing of which comes at a profound cost. *It matters how one fights*—not only for the new society a revolutionary movement hopes to build (the case of the FLN and postindependence Algeria is again instructive) but for the individual human beings who do the fighting and suffer it.

Anticolonial violence may well be "dis-intoxicating"—a sobering-up or awakening into liberatory struggle—but whatever it is, Fanon wants us to understand, there is nothing "cleansing" or "redemptive" about it. In focusing so intently and in such detail on the mental—and moral—casualties of the Algerian war, and its dehumanizing and genocidal nature, Fanon the doctor, the genuine healer, writes about his patients not in the abstract ideological and racial terms of a Manichaean anticolonialism but in terms of their individual, flesh-and-blood actuality. It is not violence that heals his patients; it is the healing care of another person.

"Why not simply try to touch the other, feel the other, discover each other?" Fanon asked in *Black Skin, White Masks*. There, and again in the final chapter of *The Wretched of the Earth*, Fanon's answer to the "zone of nonbeing"—into which his brothers and sisters, fellow human beings, are flung—is to acknowledge them in their distinct suffering, their person, their naked and irreducible human existence.

Almost as if to say, along with Arendt at the edge of the abyss in *The Origins of Totalitarianism*, citing Augustine of Hippo—now the city of Annaba on the northeastern coast of Algeria, not far from Skikda, formerly Philippeville—"I want you to be."

3.

Pardon what may seem a digression, but it has always struck me as more than just a curiosity, a bit of intellectual trivia, that Hannah Arendt wrote her 1929 doctoral dissertation on Saint Augustine. Because the central questions of that dissertation are, as she put it, "the meaning and importance of neighborly love" and how Augustine understood "the neighbor's relevance." Noting that his "every perception and every remark about love refer at least in part to this love of neighbor," Arendt observes that for Augustine the relevance of the other "was simply a matter of course." Our shared condition of "createdness," in Augustine's thinking, means that the neighbor is one's equal. One loves in the neighbor "the being that lives in him as his source," and as Arendt explains, "the same source is loved in each individual human being." Augustine saw in the "historical fact" of our common descent, and our common sinfulness inherited from Adam, "the foundation of a definite and obligatory equality among all people . . . a kinship beyond any mere likeness," Arendt writes. "The individual is not alone in this world. He has companions-in-fate . . . the situation of mortality." And not only is this the foundation of human kinship for Augustine, but of "fellowship," rooted in equality. "The explicitness of equality is contained in the commandment of neighborly love," Arendt writes. In Augustine's ideal community, the City of God, she explains, "love extends to all people."

Yet even here, writing in 1929, the young Arendt is careful to clarify in her conclusion, "love does not turn to humankind but to the individual, albeit every individual." Or again, as she would phrase it some three decades later, in *The Human Condition*, "men, not Man, live on the earth and inhabit the world." If understood as ethics, she realized, then the love of neighbor—of the other human being, fundamentally one's equal—must translate into action. And one does not act toward, just as one does not love, an abstraction. One can only act toward, as one can only truly love, a person.

Raised in a secular Jewish family, Arendt seems never to have been religiously observant in a traditional sense—she comes across as the classic agnostic, maybe because she found agnosticism the only intellectually respectable stance. But her openness and respect toward religious thought and tradition ran deep, going back to her earliest work, from her dissertation to her essays on Jewish identity in the 1930s and '40s. In a warm appreciation of Martin Buber in 1935, when she was working with young Jewish refugees in Paris, Arendt addressed assimilated German Jews like herself who had only lately been forced "to become aware of themselves *as Jews*," and found they lacked a "*Judaic* bond." (The italics are hers.) Another important Jewish scholar whose work fascinated and influenced Arendt was Gershom Scholem, especially his groundbreaking *Major Trends in Jewish Mysticism* (1941), as seen in their correspondence from the '40s and her review of the book, published in 1946, which Scholem considered one of the most perceptive it had received.

But in the fall of 1963, engulfed in the heated controversy within the Jewish world over *Eichmann in Jerusalem*—a "political campaign," as she wrote to her close friend Mary McCarthy, mobilized against her and directed at "a book which was never written"—Arendt fell out with Scholem, with whom she'd developed a bond in their shared friendship with Walter Benjamin. As it turned out, Scholem was among those outraged by the book's critical and at times, even Arendt admitted, ironic tone ("downright malicious," Scholem told her) toward the Israeli prosecution of Eichmann and, what was worse, the role during the Holocaust of some Jewish council leaders in Europe who complied with the Nazis to help facilitate deportations. ("I don't presume to judge," Scholem wrote. "I wasn't there.")

In their widely read exchange of letters on the controversy, published in January 1964 (and reprinted in the 2007 Arendt collection *The Jewish Writings*), Scholem felt it necessary to assure Arendt, "I regard you wholly as a daughter of our people, and in no other way"—as though she had ever pretended or claimed to be otherwise. Arendt responded that she found this "puzzling," as indeed it is (not to mention patronizing and patriarchal), given her very public embrace of Jewish identity in numerous articles across three decades, as well as in private correspondence with Scholem himself.

Equally strange, then, that Scholem would not only attack her for being anti-Zionist (as was well known) but also for lacking, as he put it, *Ahabath Israel*, or "love of the Jewish people." Perhaps he had not read all of Arendt's essays on Jewish politics in the 1940s and '50s, and had missed, for example, her 1948 piece in *Commentary*, "To Save the Jewish Homeland," where she wrote that the building up of such a homeland in Palestine—as distinguished from the establishment of a Jewish state, of which she was skeptical—was "the great hope and the great pride of Jews all over the world," herself included, and that its destruction would amount to a "catastrophe . . . almost beyond imagining." At the same time, she criticized the intransigent Zionist position in which "the Arabs—all Arabs—are our enemies," and called out the "plain racist chauvinism" of Zionism's "division between Jews and all other peoples." To the contrary, she wrote hopefully, "Arab–Jewish cooperation"—far from being "an idealistic daydream"—was the only realistic way forward and could "show the world that there are no differences between two peoples that cannot be bridged."

But Scholem had surely read her long 1944 essay "Zionism Reconsidered," where she had critiqued the Zionist "doctrine of eternal antisemitism"—in which a universal hostility toward Jews, "always and everywhere," functions as "some mysterious natural law," with its "assumption, as arbitrary as it is absurd, that every gentile living with Jews must become a conscious or subconscious Jew-hater"—and where she criticized "the spectacle of a national movement," having begun with such "idealistic élan," selling out to imperialist powers and showing "no solidarity with other oppressed peoples." We know that Scholem read it because he wrote to her, from his home in Jerusalem, an angry and scolding letter in response. Arendt's tense, lengthy reply, in a letter of April 1946, was as pointed as it was dignified: "To be honest," she wrote, "not even in my darkest dreams did it ever occur to me that you had a Zionist 'worldview'"—which, as she saw it, shared with other nineteenth and twentieth-century ideologies, whether nationalist or communist, "a common fanaticism, a shared screen against reality." Indeed, there was a "very real danger," she wrote, "that a consistent nationalist has no other choice but to become a racist." (We can't know precisely how Arendt would have responded to the aggressions of today's right-wing Zionist ethnonationalism, but in an open letter to *The New York Times* in December 1948, cosigned by Albert Einstein and other luminaries, she equated Israel's nascent Freedom Party led by Irgun commander Menachem Begin—future Likud founder and Israeli prime minister—with the Nazi and Fascist parties of Europe.)

Scholem, then, should not have been surprised when Arendt wrote, in their 1963 exchange over *Eichmann*, "What confuses you is that my arguments and my approach are different from what you are used to; in other words, the trouble is that I am independent." Nor should he have been surprised when, responding to his charge that she lacked a love of the Jewish people, Arendt wrote, "You are quite right—I am not moved by any 'love' of this sort," and went on to offer him two reasons. One of them was that this "love of the Jews," given that she herself was Jewish, seemed to her "rather suspect." She informed him of a conversation she had had in Israel with "a prominent political personality" (Golda Meir, in fact), who said to her, "as a Socialist, I, of course, do not believe in God; I believe in the Jewish people." Arendt found this statement "shocking," and told Scholem: "The greatness of this people was once that it believed in God and believed in Him in such a way that its trust and love toward Him was greater than its fear. And now this people believes only in itself? What good can come out of that?"

The other reason, indeed, the one she offered him first, was simply this: "I have never in my life 'loved' any people or collective—neither the German people, nor the French, nor the Americans, nor the working class or anything of that sort. I indeed love 'only' my friends and the only kind of love I know of and believe in is the love of persons."

4.

This book began with Arendt's analysis of genocidal totalitarianism and what lessons there might be for our moment of converging political and climate catastrophes. It comes to a close with a reading of Fanon—and Arendt again—in the context of another genocide, this one in Palestine, a land all but condemned on our current path to be uninhabitable due to global heating, whatever the outcome of war and negotiations over the land's occupation and liberation. All of which brings us back to the global climate struggle—integral to any hope for a future of peace and justice in Palestine, in Israel, in the Middle East as a whole, and everywhere else.

The global climate-justice struggle is not monolithic, and it never has been. There will almost certainly never be a single movement, "Fanonian" or Gandhian or Marxist or otherwise. Nor should there be. (There is much to be said for a diversity of both strategies and tactics.) The global struggle, the movement of movements, will always look like the myriad different places and communities where people are fighting for their lives, their children's lives, their neighbors' lives—their collective future. Global solidarity requires international cooperation and coordination, across cultures and faiths and ideologies, not uniformity. Solidarity is hard enough at the national and local level, within any movement or community, however small.

What, then, I must ask my staunchest comrades, would an emerging "Fanonian" movement look like today—whether for anticolonial liberation or global climate justice, or against fascism and for genuine democracy, or all of the above (as it surely must be)?

Strangely, it might have something essential in common, on some root humanistic level, with an "Arendtian" one, if that's imaginable. No pacificist, Arendt—for her there was such a thing as a just war (another principle she shared with Augustine), and yes, even revolution. What mattered was the mutual recognition of individual human worth and dignity—the basis, as Fanon would say, of human "love and understanding." Of course their ideological differences were real. But perhaps on this shared foundation a genuine communication, even solidarity, might be possible.

If violence, armed struggle, is justified in the cause of anticolonial liberation and antifascist resistance—and in spite of my own nonviolent commitments (in solidarity with my overwhelmingly nonviolent comrades), it is hard to argue that it is not—then how could it not be justified in the struggle against global, neocolonial, fossil-fuel driven ecocide amounting to genocide in many of the world's poorest and most oppressed places? Against the willful—because foreseeable and preventable—decimation, if not eradication, of entire populations and cultures rendered "superfluous" by totalitarian fossil capital?

As in the history of anticolonial liberation struggles, the climate-justice struggle—the fight for a habitable planet and a livable human future in which justice is still possible—will not be radical enough, or fearless enough, until enough of us are *desperate enough* to risk everything. We may yet dis-intoxicate ourselves. The question, maybe the only question left at this hour, is whether we will hold on to our humanity in our desperation.

"While this everywhere crying"

Jane Hirshfield, Poet of the Present Moment

DECEMBER 2023

Throughout the night   song after song
How can I   speak at dawn.
—Su Tung-p'o, translated by Gary Snyder, "We Wash Our
   Bowls in This Water," *Mountains and Rivers Without End*
   (1996)

Dawn after dawn one night only, we woke in your arms.
—Jane Hirshfield, "Aubade Now of Earth" (2022)

It was late September 2022, and I was on my way to visit Jane
Hirshfield—but first I had to get to Stinson Beach without driving off a cliff into the pitch-dark Pacific. The fog was thick along
the high, snaking coastal road at the base of Mount Tamalpais,
and the headlights of my rented Prius (fraudulent signal of a personal virtue I've never possessed) weren't cutting it. With each
curve I hugged the mountain, keeping as far as possible from the

abyss of mist, rock, and watery vastness. It was, I admit, a little scary. Somehow I managed to stay on the road.

Soon enough, tiny Stinson emerged out of nowhere, its few streetlights making circles in the fog. Being late, I found my room key in an envelope taped to the office door of the little motor inn a short walk from the beach. I needed sleep, but my nervous system was still out on the cliffs.

Jane and I have corresponded occasionally for many years—since the 1990s, when I was a twentysomething editor at a national magazine—and we had met in person once before, too briefly, at a book festival in 2015. This time, I was visiting friends in the Bay Area, and I had reached out to Jane beforehand to see if she'd be at home in Mill Valley. She said she would and that she'd be delighted to get together some afternoon while I was there. She suggested we meet at the horse stables in Muir Beach and then walk the trail to Green Gulch Farm Zen Center. As a longtime Zen Buddhist practitioner (although with nowhere near Jane's five decades of experience, including her three years of monastic training at Tassajara), I'd heard about Green Gulch, which is affiliated with the San Francisco Zen Center, and was eager to see it. So that was the plan: We'd walk, talk, maybe sit in the Green Gulch garden, and catch up.

I had no assignment and wasn't pursuing one. This was personal. I had read Jane's recent volume, *Ledger* (2020), and some of the new poems in *The Asking: New and Selected Poems* (then still a year from publication), and I was struck—no, I was startled, unsettled, caught, seen—by the increasingly grave urgency and grief of her clear-sighted ecological witness.

That next morning in Stinson, before meeting Jane in the afternoon, I woke up early and headed down to the water. It was overcast and pleasantly cool, not socked in like the night before.

Still, the marine layer hid all but the first few hundred feet of the mountain. The beach at Stinson is long and wide, in a broad arc along Bolinas Bay, and at the southeast end, where I was, the center of town is set back at a respectful distance. Aside from a few early swimmers far up the beach, I was alone with the sand and the shorebirds and the small, quiet surf. A long-billed curlew posed for me on its twigs-for-legs in the inch-deep foam of a spent wave. A group of marbled godwits (as I later ascertained) took flight low above the water and landed a few yards out in front of me. A thick flock of gulls huddled on the sand. I walked the half mile or so down to the photogenic boulders at the end of the beach, below the coast road I'd driven, beyond the town and any buildings. The wet, immaculate sand reflected the early light, and the big rocks emerged from its surface as if they'd grown from it.

The ocean itself, calm and metallic gray under the blanket of low cloud, went on absorbing the atmosphere's excess heat and carbon dioxide—warming, rising, acidifying, silently and invisibly, so as not to alarm the tourists like me.

§

Ledger begins with a poem called "Let Them Not Say"—the poem's "them" left somewhat ambiguous, whether it's the deniers of various sorts, the oblivious, the cynical, or, perhaps in the end, posterity, incredulous and judging:

> Let them not say: we did not see it.
> We saw.
>
> Let them not say: we did not hear it.
> We heard.

Let them not say: they did not taste it.
We ate, we trembled.

Let them not say: it was not spoken, not written.
We spoke,
we witnessed with voices and hands.

Let them not say: they did nothing.
We did not-enough.

Let them say, as they must say something:

A kerosene beauty.
It burned.

Let them say we warmed ourselves by it,
read by its light, praised,
and it burned.

The spare lyricism here, a piercing directness and clarity, is pure Hirshfield. And yet there's something else, too: a stark reckoning, a depth of anger, an incalculable grief, an ending, an abyss. This felt new to me.

Clearly, as anyone who knows me or has read the essays in this book is aware, I'm no stranger to the mood of grief and doom that has settled like smoke-haze over so many of us who pay attention to climate science and our ecological and political catastrophes. As a journalist and an activist, having fought pipelines and blockaded coal trains, I've stared straight into that abyss for a decade and a half. I know despair; we're on intimate terms, and I won't be shamed for it. (We're told it's a sin.) You can't run from it—you may think you can, but it catches up with you.

In the months before my trip to California, I'd been wrestling hard with this mixture of climate and political despair, and I shared my thoughts with Jane before my visit. Her reply was typically generous.

"I actually believe in despair," she wrote in an email, "though it's possible that what I mean by that word is not what the despair-condemners mean by it. They mean: the collapse to nihilism, paralysis, Nero-ism. I mean something like: admit the abyss is real and truly may swallow us all, because only then will we do whatever we can to prevent it. Perhaps this isn't despair, in the strictest sense. Perhaps despair is a full giving up. But for me it feels like despair: an unbearable pitch into falling and darkness. In my experience, only the full admission into heart and mind of the depths of foreseeable collapse is sufficient as a spur to not giving up. And to not being complacent, to not assume that others, somehow, will take care of the problem for us."

There's another poem in *Ledger*, in that volume's final section, in which Jane transmutes those sentiments into art. Called "Ghazal for the End of Time," it was inspired by Olivier Messiaen's *Quartet for the End of Time*—his disquieting yet somehow enrapturing piece for clarinet, piano, violin, and cello—composed and first performed in a Nazi prison camp. Here it is in full:

Ghazal for the End of Time

(after Messiaen)

Break anything—a window, a piecrust, a glacier—it will break open.
A voice cannot speak, cannot sing, without lips, teeth, lamina propria
    coming open.

Some breakage can barely be named, hardly be spoken.

Rains stopped, roof said. Fires, forests, cities, cellars peeled open.

Tears stopped, eyes said. An unhearable music fell instead from them.
A clarinet stripped of its breathing, the cello abandoned.

The violin grieving, a hand too long empty held open.
The imperial piano, its 89th, 90th, 91st strings unsummoned,
     unwoken.

Watching, listening, was like that: the low, wordless humming of
     being unwoven.
Fish vanished. Bees vanished. Bats whitened. Arctic ice opened.

Hands wanted more time, hands thought we had time. Spending
     time's rivers,
its meadows, its mountains, its instruments tuning their silence, its
     deep mantle broken.

Earth stumbled within and outside us.
Orca, thistle, kestrel withheld their instruction.

Rock said, Burning Ones, pry your own blindness open.
Death said, Now I too am orphan.

"That poem frightened me profoundly—especially the ending,"
Jane wrote to me not long after I saw her in California. "I think it
the darkest poem I've ever written."

"I've long loved Messiaen's piece," Jane wrote. "I find it over-
poweringly beautiful. But not as Messiaen described his intentions
for it. He claimed that he was praising the radiance of God, percep-
tible even from prison camp. But I hear in it infinite grief, a grief
hauntingly beautiful, not transcendence. I am perhaps wrong. (I

wonder how you yourself hear it?) But a person hears what she does."

I asked her about that grief. She likened it to the Latin *lacrimae rerum* ("tears of things") or the Japanese *mono no aware* ("pathos of things," or the awareness of transience). "Perhaps it is only my not-enlightened human disposition," she wrote, "though it's also the disposition of Greek tragedies, and of Japanese poems: a beauty unaccompanied by grief, impermanence-knowledge, mortality, seems to me almost instantly saccharine."

"My 'end of time' in this poem," she explained, "borrows Messiaen's phrase for a different use and meaning. His was theological (and I can't help but think, personal, given its circumstances of composition). My poem has in mind only the crisis of the biosphere, the possibility that the world you and I were born into might be coming to a close."

I told her the poem's darkness is indeed unlike anything of hers I'd read before—and yet, I also sensed something life-affirming in it. There's an affirmation, even defiance, perhaps a kind of human solidarity, in her resolve to face her fear and grief and turn it into art: a hard acceptance and a fierce resistance. "Rock said, Burning Ones, pry your own blindness open"—the monosyllabic force of the verb "pry," like a sudden, almost violent rupture. "Death said, Now I too am orphan"—the final, dying downbeat of the last half-rhyme, the sound of fate, impermanence, falling. All as if to say: "Resist, you fools!—now!—in this one moment that is all you have." Even as, in the end, death itself is swallowed by eternity.

§

Jane Hirshfield is not ordinarily grouped and anthologized with poets of political engagement and social witness. Among the most distinguished living poets in the English language, she's best known for her quiet, contemplative attention to the natural world, to the details of daily life; for finding the profound in the mundane, the mystical (but never supernatural) in the materiality of existence—an openhearted relationship to the large and small that is both broader and more vulnerable than the labels "Zen" and "Buddhist" can encompass. ("I don't want to be a 'Zen' poet, only a human poet," she told me.) Her verse is cerebral and sensual, somehow both philosophical and anti-philosophical at the same time. Abstract concepts and questions are constantly met with and grounded in tangible, earthy, embodied reality, so that a single line might enact the tension or balance, like dance or musical counterpoint, between the intellectual, physical, and emotional. All with the clarity of sun on snowmelt.

Jane was born and raised in New York City, yet her earliest memory—"now a memory of a memory of a memory," she told me—is of a trip to the countryside, maybe her first, when she was about two years old: "lying in the grass with a tall, dark hedge behind me, blue sky up above, and the taste of a blackberry in my mouth." It's like an uncanny ur-image of a Hirshfield poem, an awakening before words into what would be her life's work, her poetry of the present moment.

And yet, Jane pointed out to me when I saw her again in June—as we sat on a terrace in upstate New York and looked through the bound proofs of *The Asking*—political and social awareness has never been absent from her work. What, then, are Jane Hirshfield's politics? I asked her that question as we sat talking about the new book.

"My politics are the politics of nonseparation," she said. "If I could find a way to move us all out of meaning anything other than all of us when we say 'we,' that's my politics. The politics of classic Mahayana Buddhism: lessen suffering. Whatever will make for less suffering, whatever will make for less tribalism, and the sense that any person's abundance comes only at someone else's expense. My belief is that when people experience their lives as abundant and not under threat, our natural response is generosity, is sharing, is 'Have you eaten yet?'—and that this is in us as a species, to behave badly under threat and well when we have a sense of abundance. The politics of that have to do with: How can we cultivate a sense of abundance which is not tied to the false separation of 'I own this'?"

"And, you know, human beings have lived this way," she continued, "it's not out of our repertoire to live with a sense of shared abundance. Our current culture doesn't cultivate that very well. Our current culture creates a great fearfulness, and I feel like it is a generous accident of my own life that I am not trapped inside that. If I had been born somewhere else under different circumstances, I might not be able to feel this."

We had talked about my own activism at the more confrontational edge of the climate justice movement, and I was curious to know how she views her relationship to radical politics and social justice movements.

"I came of age during the Vietnam War protests," she wrote to me after our conversation in New York. "I took a train to the DC Mall and sat with others my last year in high school. In college, I fasted a week to protest the bombing of Cambodia and sent the money [I saved on food] to some fund, meant to help. I always thought a life could only be felt honorable if you'd spent a night in jail for reasons of justice. My life is not yet honorable, by that measure."

"I know how much I am not doing—I mean, politically," she told me. "I write a lot of postcards these days, to help get people registered to vote."

In fact, she does a good bit more than write voter postcards (important work in itself). In 2017, she founded Poets for Science to coincide with the March for Science in Washington, DC—and read her searing poem "On the Fifth Day," about the silencing of environmental scientists (which had just run as a full page in *The Washington Post*) to a crowd of more than forty thousand. She participated in a Nobel Science Summit on countering misinformation and restoring public trust in science.

"Not a jail cell, not silence," she noted in self-judgment. "I'm grateful for those who are more radical in their actions. My way of working for change is quieter."

On that porch in New York, the smoke of Canadian wildfires in the air, we came back to the crisis of the biosphere. I told her that I don't think we will ever do what actually needs to be done, something like revolution, until enough people are desperate enough—a frightening thought. This led us back to our conversation about climate and political despair, and the fear of it.

"Two or three years ago," Jane said, "I noticed there was this great turn, and people who'd been talking about how bad things are getting decided they had to start talking and writing about hope."

Yes, I said, I had noticed. It bothered me.

"Well," she said, "their fear of despair is honorable and justified, because what they're afraid of is the teenagers who are killing themselves."

I get that, of course, especially as a parent. What I resist, I told her, is the culture of browbeating optimism that has overtaken large parts of the climate movement. It does young people no favors in the end because it avoids the necessary reckoning with reality.

Yes, she nodded. "That can be kind of obnoxious and programmatic."

She paused. "I always want to be on the side of understanding where people are coming from," Jane said. And then the conversation took an unexpected turn.

"There was one time in my life," she said, her soft voice getting softer, "when I was in—and I only realized it when I had come out, it had no name when I was in it—a full-bore, clinical depression. And it was long-lasting, and it was perilous. This was in 1982—my first great love ended things abruptly, and it threw me over a cliff. I was there for a long time, and I got out, and I'm not sure—I don't know if I would survive if I ever had to go there again."

"I'm deeply glad that I have experienced it," she said. "Because, first of all, it made me a larger human being, just in terms of what I've experienced. And now, if someone else is in the abyss—I know that. It's not just words to me. Because I lived there."

"This all has to do with people who are pushing despair away," she continued. "Perhaps too quickly and superficially, because they're afraid to actually feel it. I think it's very important to feel it—and it's very important to not kill yourself."

Those last words she spoke quietly, slowly, emphatically.

"This is still a beautiful world," she said. "It's not yet a Cormac McCarthy nightmare."

Although large parts of it will be, I said. Some places already are.

"Oh, yes," she said. "Some places already are."

§

I didn't tell Jane this, because I don't talk about it much, but I've been there, where Jane was, in recent years—all the way there. And I fear it. I'd rather go to prison, or die, fighting fossil fuels and fascists than go back to that place—to feel the vertigo, the over-the-cliff, into-the-abyss free fall.

Someone might say, in fact I myself have been known to say, that people like Jane, including a lot of people in the climate movement—well-educated, mainly white, relatively privileged Americans like myself, and especially those of a political and intellectual bent—are not doing nearly enough, unwilling to take the kinds of risks that are necessary. I've said that words are cheap at this late hour—especially words like "hope" and "not too late"—and that direct action and a readiness to make sacrifices are now what matters. And I still believe all of that—even as I struggle to live up to it.

And yet, if it were not for certain poems of Jane Hirshfield and a few others—Han Shan and Su Tung-p'o, Shih-wu and Muso, Snyder and Merwin—I, for one, might very well not be here. I might not have made it to the other side. Who am I to say she's not doing "enough"? She may have saved my life.

Am I doing *enough*? Is anyone?

Among the new poems in *The Asking* is one titled "Manifest," in which Jane writes: "To that which is coming, I say, / Here, take what is yours." And she goes on to address the "what-is-coming" ("glaciers depart, insects quiet, seas rise") as if addressing a person: "But forget, if you can, what-is-coming . . . / one small handful of moments and gestures. . . . // Let stay, if you can, what-is-coming, / one or two musical notes. . . ." Until the poem ends:

> Leave one unfraudulent hope,
> one affection like curtains blown open in wind,
> whose minutes, seconds, fragrance,
> choices,
> won't sadden the heart to recall.

To call this fatalism would be too easy, a kind of evasion. To admit despair at the knowledge of what is coming and what will be lost—and what is lost already—is not fatalism; it's a kind of maturity, emotional honesty, sanity.

In the last of *The Asking*'s new poems, "I Open the Window," Jane describes a restless night and tells us that it's not the rain or the cold that she wanted to let in, but "the siren, the thunder, the neighbor, / the fireworks, the dog's bark. // Which of them didn't matter?" Which leads her to conclude, defiantly, "Yes, this world is perfect, / all things as they are" (a reference to Buddhist teaching):

> But I wanted
> not to be
> the one sleeping soundly, on a soft pillow,
> clean sheets untroubled,
> dreaming there still might be time,
>
> while this everywhere crying

§

That afternoon in September, I met Jane as planned at the stables in Muir Beach. When I arrived, I saw her small figure in the corral, wearing faded jeans and an olive fleece with a California State Parks Volunteer patch on the arm. Flame, her dark chestnut gelding, companion of twenty-six years, trotted gamely around the ring. Flame died on the winter solstice, she later told me. "Throughout his life, until the end, we just got closer and closer."

We walked the short trail over to the farm and the Zen center, officially known as Green Dragon Temple, founded in the early 1970s in the rugged ravine of Green Gulch. I don't remember much of our conversation, though we talked for more than two hours, sitting on a comfortable bench in a hedge-enclosed garden between fields and zendo. I do remember telling her how another of her more recent poems had stuck in my head. It's called "Aubade Now of Earth," an aubade being a song or poem of lovers parting at dawn, and it has remained with me alongside her "Ghazal," repeated countless times, a sort of *gatha* (in Buddhist practice, a verse recited in rhythm with the breath):

Aubade Now of Earth

Sun on it again, at first tender.
The color of apricots ripening into.

At first there was more to eat, then suddenly less.

For one night only, naked in my arms,
wrote Beatriz of Dia, in twelfth-century Occitan,
to her longed-for lover.

Aubade now of earth. Of water. Of herons and fishes.

Dawn after dawn one night only, we woke in your arms.

This, too, notwithstanding its spacious and supple lyricism, is a rather dark poem—even if it describes sunrise. And yet it's nothing like the darkness of her "Ghazal." It seems to come from a similar place, but something else is driving it. After my visit, I asked Jane in an email: What is it that saves "Aubade" from the abyss of "Ghazal"?

"You have 'Aubade' just right," she wrote to me. "It too foresees the end of this world you and I were born into—but praises it for having existed in all its beauty more than it mourns what we have done to it. Isn't it the same for the lover departing at dawn? That night of love will never return. But it did happen, and that cannot be undone."

The day after our talk at Green Gulch, I took another early walk on Stinson Beach, then hiked to the top of Mount Tam, up through the fog until I got above the trees and clouds and saw the sun. It was dry as death up there—the toll of long drought—but from somewhere deep in the mountain, water still flowed.

CODA

What am I doing? Can this be real?

In that moment I am walking down railroad tracks in moonlight, surrounded by dense woods, in the small, still hours long before dawn. The tracks ahead of me extend into the dark, my eyes playing tricks, shapes emerging in the shadows—wolf? Cop?

In the distance the glowing lights of the power plant, fired by coal, seen so many times from this vantage—mundane, chilling—the smokestack plume floating, illuminated by the moon, absorbed into a clear night sky.

I follow the tracks into the back of the plant, where mountains of coal—acrid, choking dust and rock—stand dimly silhouetted, and past the hulking, silent, ghostly mass of freight cars, coal hoppers. Farther into the plant, toward the eerie glow in the distance through the pines, alert for the headlights of the security guard on his rounds, past the shed and machinery where they unload the coal freight, add it to the infernal pile. I see the conveyors and escalators that move the coal upward along aerial structures like some dystopian theme-park ride and into the tall unit where it's crushed into finer particles, then out and along more conveyors and into the plant's inner works.

How exposed, vulnerable. Doors unlocked. Machinery accessible.

I keep to the shadows and approach the pumphouse where cooling water from the adjacent river is drawn through large pipes and into the plant. Lights on inside. I open the door. Nobody home.

I'm in the control room, rows of panels, buttons and blinking lights—am I in a movie, a dream, or am I really doing this?

On the wall by the door, I find what I'm looking for, the power source, the electrical box, the shutoff switch . . . in case of emergency . . .

No need to blow up anything, nothing spectacular, no one in danger (everyone in danger) . . . just a surgical operation . . . to disarm a weapon of mass destruction . . . in case of emergency . . .

How easy. How hard. How impossibly hard. And yet how easy.

ACKNOWLEDGMENTS

Essays, even the personal ones, are collaborative endeavors, and I'm immensely grateful to all the editors at the publications where these essays originally appeared in earlier form (some with different titles), and especially Evan Kindley at *Los Angeles Review of Books*, Dave Denison at *The Baffler*, and Roane Carey, Don Guttenplan, and Katrina vanden Heuvel at *The Nation*.

Los Angeles Review of Books: "Learning to Live in the Dark" (September 22, 2017). In addition, a small portion of chapter 9 originally appeared, in slightly different form, in "No Safe Options: A Conversation with Andreas Malm" (January 5, 2021).

The Baffler: "Carbon Ironies" (June 13, 2018), "The Social Beast" (April 14, 2021), "Great Sinners" (March 2022), "The Rebel" (September 15, 2022), "Risk and Revolution" (July 20, 2023).

The Nation: "Living in Truth" (April 11, 2019), "The Hardest Thing" (October 12, 2020), "Walden at Midnight" (August 23/30, 2021), "How to Blow Up a Climate Fantasy" (November 19, 2022, and April 17/24, 2023), "While this everywhere crying" (December 11/18, 2023).

The poems by Jane Hirshfield ("Let Them Not Say," "Ghazal for the End of Time," and "Aubade Now of Earth"), from *Ledger: Poems* (Knopf, 2020) and *The Asking: New and Selected Poems* (Knopf, 2023), are used by permission of Jane Hirshfield.

"Walden at Midnight" was originally commissioned for the anthology *Now Comes Good Sailing: Writers Reflect on Henry David Thoreau*, edited by Andrew Blauner (Princeton University Press,

October 2021), where it first appeared in book form.

"The Desperate of the Earth," written in the summer of 2024, is published here for the first time.

§

I finished this book with a mixture of gratitude, astonishment, and some regret. The regret is simply for all the ways the book inevitably falls short of the ideal—its imperfections and limitations, all of which are my mine alone. The astonishment is that the book exists at all, that I was somehow able to write it. But most of all, there is gratitude that it will be published, that someone saw fit to put their imprint on it, marshal their resources, and send it out into the world, come what may.

And so I'm profoundly grateful to John McDonald, my editor at Haymarket Books. This book wouldn't exist without John's belief in it, and it benefited in many ways from his keen questions, insights, and comradely prodding. My deepest gratitude also goes to Anthony Arnove, to Haymarket's editorial board, and to each and every person at Haymarket Books, for keeping the radical flame alive.

There are many people who helped me get through the years covered in this book. I can't list them all (some are strangers who simply showed me kindness), but foremost among them are Dr. Robert Torchin, Rev. Kate Malin, Rev. Garrett Yates, Zen Master Bon Haeng (Mark Houghton), and friends in the faith and activist communities to which I belong. Most of all, my sisters, who have always been there for me.

At the end of the day, and the start of the next one, I wouldn't be able to do any of this work without the amazing love and support of my life partner, Fiona. Our children, Duncan and Grace—you are why I go on fighting.

SELECTED BIBLIOGRAPHY

Prelude: "Truly, I live in dark times!"

Arendt, Hannah. *Men in Dark Times*. New York: Harcourt Brace & Company, 1968.

Brecht, Bertolt. *The Collected Poems of Bertolt Brecht*. Translated and edited by Tom Kuhn and David Constantine. New York: Liveright, 2019.

———. *Poems, 1913–1956*. Edited by John Willett and Ralph Manheim. New York: Methuen, 1976.

Learning to Live in the Dark

Arendt, Hannah. *Eichmann in Jerusalem: A Report on the Banality of Evil*. New York: Penguin Books, 2006.

———. *Essays in Understanding, 1930–1954: Formation, Exile, and Totalitarianism*. Edited by Jerome Kohn. New York: Schocken Books, 1994.

———. *The Human Condition*. Second Edition. Chicago: University of Chicago Press, 1998.

———. *Men in Dark Times*. New York: Harcourt Brace & Company, 1968.

———. *The Origins of Totalitarianism*. New York: Harcourt, 1968.

———. *Responsibility and Judgment*. Edited by Jerome Kohn. New York: Schocken Books, 2003.

Camus, Albert. *Neither Victims Nor Executioners: An Ethic Superior to Murder*. Translated by Dwight Macdonald. Eugene, OR: Wipf and Stock, 2007.

Neiman, Susan. *Evil in Modern Thought: An Alternative History of Philosophy*. Princeton, NJ: Princeton University Press, 2015.

Stangneth, Bettina. *Eichmann Before Jerusalem: The Unexamined Life of a Mass Murderer*. Translated by Ruth Martin. New York: Alfred E. Knopf, 2014.

Young-Bruehl, Elisabeth. *Hannah Arendt: For Love of the World*. Second Edition. New Haven: Yale University Press, 2004.

Carbon Ironies

Scranton, Roy. *Learning to Die in the Anthropocene: Reflections on the End of a Civilization*. San Francisco: City Lights Books, 2015.

Vollmann, William T. *Carbon Ideologies, Volume I: No Immediate Danger*. New York: Viking, 2018.

———. *Carbon Ideologies, Volume II: No Good Alternative*. New York: Viking, 2018.

———. *Poor People*. New York: HarperCollins, 2008.

———. *Rising Up and Rising Down*. New York: HarperCollins, 2005.

Living in Truth

Havel, Václav. *Open Letters: Selected Writings, 1965–1990*. Edited by Paul Wilson. New York: Vintage Books, 1992.

Intergovernmental Panel on Climate Change (IPCC). Special Report: Warming of 1.5 C. Geneva: IPCC, 2018.

Judt, Tony. *Postwar: A History of Europe Since 1945*. New York: The Penguin Press, 2005.

Klein, Naomi. *No Is Not Enough: Resisting Trump's Shock Politics and Winning the World We Need*. Chicago: Haymarket Books, 2017.

———. *This Changes Everything: Capitalism vs. the Climate*. New York: Simon & Schuster, 2014.

Leiserowitz, Anthony, et al. *Climate Activism: Beliefs, Attitudes, and Behaviors – November 2019*. Yale University and George Mason University. New Haven, CT: Yale Program on Climate Change Communication, 2019.

McKibben, Bill. *The End of Nature*. New York: Random House, 2006.

———. *Falter: Has the Human Game Begun to Play Itself Out?* New York: Henry Holt, 2019.

———. "How the Active Many Can Overcome the Ruthless Few." *The Nation*, December 19–26, 2016.

Steffen, Alex. "The Real Politics of the Planetary Crisis." *The Nearly Now*, Medium.com, December 8, 2017.

Stephenson, Wen. "Against Climate Barbarism: A Conversation with Naomi Klein." *Los Angeles Review of Books*, September 30, 2019.

————. *What We're Fighting for Now Is Each Other: Dispatches From the Front Lines of Climate Justice*. Boston: Beacon Press, 2015.

Wallace-Wells, David. *The Uninhabitable Earth: Life After Warming*. New York: Tim Duggan Books, 2019.

The Hardest Thing

Freeman, John, ed. *Tales of Two Planets: Stories of Climate Change and Inequality in a Divided World*. New York: Penguin Books, 2020.

Girgenti, Guido and Varshini Prakash, eds. *Winning the Green New Deal: Why We Must, How We Can*. New York: Simon and Schuster, 2020.

Interlude: Walden at Midnight

Thoreau, Henry D. *Collected Essays and Poems*. New York: Library of America, 2001.

————. *Henry David Thoreau: A Week on the Concord and Merrimack Rivers / Walden; Or, Life in the Woods / The Maine Woods / Cape Cod*. New York: Library of America, 1985.

————. *The Journal, 1837–1861*. Edited by Damion Searls. New York: New York Review Books, 2009.

Richardson, Robert D. *Henry Thoreau: A Life of the Mind*. Berkeley, CA: University of California Press, 1986.

Walls, Laura Dassow. *Henry David Thoreau: A Life*. Chicago: University of Chicago Press, 2017.

The Social Beast

Gray, Francine du Plessix. *Simone Weil*. Penguin Lives. New York: Viking, 2001.

Jacobs, Alan. *The Year of Our Lord 1943: Christian Humanism in an Age of Crisis*. New York: Oxford University Press, 2018.

Pétrement, Simone. *Simone Weil: A Life*. Translated by Raymond Rosenthal. New York: Random House, 1976.

Weil, Simone. *Gravity and Grace*. Translated by Emma Crawford and Mario von der Ruhr. London: Routledge, 2002.

————. *The Need for Roots: Prelude to a Declaration of Duties towards Mankind*. Translated by Arthur Wills. London: Routledge, 2002.

————. *On the Abolition of All Political Parties*. Translated by Simon Leys. New York: New York Review Books, 2013.

————. *Selected Essays, 1934-1943: Historical, Political, and Moral Writings*. Translated by Richard Rees. Eugene, OR: Wipf and Stock, 2015.

————. *Waiting for God*. Translated by Emma Craufurd. New York: Harper Perennial, 2009.

Zaretsky, Robert. *A Life Worth Living: Albert Camus and the Quest for Meaning*. Cambridge, MA: Harvard University Press, 2016.

————. *The Subversive Simone Weil: A Life in Five Ideas*. Chicago: University of Chicago Press, 2021.

Great Sinners

Dostoevsky, Fyodor M. *The Brothers Karamazov*. Translated by Richard Pevear and Larissa Volokhonsky. New York: Farrar, Straus and Giroux, 1990, 2002.

————. *Crime and Punishment*. Translated by Richard Pevear and Larissa Volokhonsky. New York: Vintage, 1993.

————. *Demons*. Translated by Richard Pevear and Larissa Volokhonsky. New York: Vintage, 1995.

————. *The Idiot*. Translated by Richard Pevear and Larissa Volokhonsky. New York: Vintage, 2003.

————. *Notes From a Dead House*. Translated by Richard Pevear and Larissa Volokhonsky. New York: Vintage, 2016.

————. *Notes From Underground*. Translated by Richard Pevear and Larissa Volokhonsky. New York: Vintage, 1994.

————. *A Writer's Diary*. Abridged Edition. Edited by Gary Saul Morson. Translated by Kenneth Lantz. Evanston, IL: Northwestern University Press, 2009.

Frank, Joseph. *Dostoevsky: A Writer in His Time*. Princeton, NJ: Princeton University Press, 2010.

Kaufman, Andrew D. *The Gambler Wife: A True Story of Love, Risk, and the Woman Who Saved Dostoyevsky*. New York: Penguin, 2021.

The Rebel

Camus, Albert. *Algerian Chronicles.* Edited by Alice Kaplan. Translated by Arthur Goldhammer. Cambridge, MA: Harvard University Press, 2014.

———. *Caligula and Three Other Plays.* Translated by Stuart Gilbert. New York: Vintage, 1958.

———. *Camus at Combat: Writing 1944-1947.* Edited by Jacqueline Lévi-Valensi. Translated by Arthur Goldhammer. Princeton, NJ: Princeton University Press, 2007.

———. *The First Man.* Translated by David Hapgood. New York: Vintage, 1996.

———. *The Myth of Sisyphus and Other Essays.* Translated by Justin O'Brien. New York: Vintage, 1991.

———. *Neither Victims Nor Executioners: An Ethic Superior to Murder.* Translated by Dwight Macdonald. Eugene, OR: Wipf and Stock, 2007.

———. *The Plague.* Translated by Laura Marris. New York: Knopf, 2021.

———. *The Rebel: An Essay on Man in Revolt.* Translated by Anthony Bower. New York: Vintage, 1959.

———. *Resistance, Rebellion, and Death: Essays.* Translated by Justin O'Brien. New York: Vintage, 1995.

———. *Speaking Out: Lectures and Speeches, 1937-1958.* Translated by Quintin Hoare. New York: Vintage, 2021.

———. *The Stranger.* Translated by Matthew Ward. New York: Vintage, 1989.

Horne, Alistair. *A Savage War of Peace: Algeria 1954-1962.* New York: New York Review Books, 2006.

Meagher, Robert. *Albert Camus and the Human Crisis.* New York: Pegasus Books, 2021.

Sartre, Jean-Paul. "Introduction." In *The Wretched of the Earth,* by Frantz Fanon. New York: Grove Press, 2004.

Todd, Olivier. *Albert Camus: A Life.* Translated by Benjamin Ivry. Carroll & Graf, 2000.

Zaretsky, Robert. *A Life Worth Living: Albert Camus and the Quest for Meaning.* Cambridge, MA: Harvard University Press, 2016.

How to Blow Up a Climate Fantasy

Intergovernmental Panel on Climate Change. Climate Change 2023: Synthesis Report. Geneva: IPCC, 2023.

———. Special Report: Warming of 1.5 C. Geneva: IPCC, 2018.

International Energy Agency (IEA). Net Zero by 2050. Paris: IEA, 2021.

Kindig, Jessie, ed. *Property Will Cost Us the Earth: Direct Action and the Future of the Global Climate Movement.* New York: Verso Books, 2022.

Malm, Andreas. *How to Blow Up a Pipeline.* New York: Verso Books, 2021.

Stephenson, Wen. "No Safe Options: A Conversation with Andreas Malm." *Los Angeles Review of Books*, January 5, 2021.

Wallace-Wells, David. "Beyond Catastrophe: A New Climate Reality Is Coming into View." *The New York Times Magazine*, October 26, 2022.

Risk and Revolution

Allinson, Jamie; Miéville, China; Seymour, Richard; Warren, Rosie; and the Salvage Collective. *The Tragedy of the Worker: Towards the Proletarocene.* New York: Verso Books, 2021.

Malm, Andreas. *Corona, Climate, Chronic Emergency: War Communism in the 21st Century.* New York: Verso Books, 2020.

———. *Fossil Capital: The Rise of Steam Power and the Roots of Global Warming.* New York: Verso Books, 2016.

———. *How to Blow Up a Pipeline.* New York: Verso Books, 2021.

Malm, Andreas and the Zetkin Collective. *White Skin, Black Fuel: On the Danger of Fossil Fascism.* New York: Verso Books, 2021.

Miéville, China. *October: The Story of the Russian Revolution.* New York: Verso Books, 2017.

———. *A Spectre, Haunting: On* The Communist Manifesto. Chicago: Haymarket Books, 2022.

Stephenson, Wen. "No Safe Options: A Conversation with Andreas Malm." *Los Angeles Review of Books*, January 5, 2021.

———. *What We're Fighting for Now Is Each Other: Dispatches from the Front Lines of Climate Justice.* Boston: Beacon Press, 2015.

Traverso, Enzo. *Left-Wing Melancholia: Marxism, History, and Memory.* New York: Columbia University Press, 2017.

———. *Revolution: An Intellectual History*. New York: Verso Books, 2021.

The Desperate of the Earth

Arendt, Hannah. *The Jewish Writings*. Edited by Jerome Kohn and Ron H. Feldman. New York: Schocken Books, 2007.

———. *On Violence*. New York: HarperCollins, 1970.

———. *Love and Saint Augustine*. Edited by Joanna Vecchiarelli Scott and Judith Chelius Stark. Chicago: University of Chicago Press, 1996.

Arendt, Hannah and Gershom Scholem. *The Correspondence of Hannah Arendt and Gershom Scholem*. Edited by Marie Luise Knott. Translated by Anthony David. Chicago: University of Chicago Press, 2017.

Baconi, Tareq. *Hamas Contained: The Rise and Pacification of Palestinian Resistance*. Stanford, CA: Stanford University Press, 2018.

———. "What Was Hamas Thinking?" *Foreign Policy*, Nov. 22, 2023.

Fanon, Frantz. *Black Skin, White Masks*. Translated by Richard Philcox. New York: Grove Press, 2008.

———. *The Wretched of the Earth*. Translated by Richard Philcox. New York: Grove Press, 2004.

Horne, Alistair. *A Savage War of Peace: Algeria 1954–1962*. New York: New York Review Books, 2006.

Macey, David. *Frantz Fanon: A Biography*. New York: Verso Books, 2012.

Said, Edward. *Culture and Imperialism*. New York: Vintage Books, 1994.

Shatz, Adam. *The Rebel's Clinic: The Revolutionary Lives of Frantz Fanon*. New York: Farrar, Straus and Giroux, 2024.

Postlude: "While this everywhere crying"

Hirshfield, Jane. *The Asking: New and Selected Poems*. New York: Knopf, 2023.

———. *Ledger: Poems*. New York: Knopf, 2020.

About the Author

Wen Stephenson is a veteran journalist, essayist, and climate-justice activist. A correspondent for *The Nation* and frequent contributor to *The Baffler*, he is the author previously of *What We're Fighting for Now Is Each Other* about the pivotal early years of the US climate-justice movement. He is a former editor at *The Atlantic* and *The Boston Globe*, where he edited the Sunday Ideas section, and has written for those and many other publications, including *Slate*, *The New York Times Book Review*, *Los Angeles Review of Books*, the *Boston Phoenix*, and elsewhere.

In 2010, he left his career in mainstream media and has since covered, engaged in, and helped organize nonviolent resistance to fossil capital.

He lives near Boston.

About Haymarket Books

Haymarket Books is a radical, independent, nonprofit book publisher based in Chicago. Our mission is to publish books that contribute to struggles for social and economic justice. We strive to make our books a vibrant and organic part of social movements and the education and development of a critical, engaged, and internationalist Left.

We take inspiration and courage from our namesakes, the Haymarket Martyrs, who gave their lives fighting for a better world. Their 1886 struggle for the eight-hour day—which gave us May Day, the international workers' holiday—reminds workers around the world that ordinary people can organize and struggle for their own liberation. These struggles—against oppression, exploitation, environmental devastation, and war—continue today across the globe.

Since our founding in 2001, Haymarket has published more than nine hundred titles. Radically independent, we seek to drive a wedge into the risk-averse world of corporate book publishing. Our authors include Angela Y. Davis, Arundhati Roy, Keeanga-Yamahtta Taylor, Eve Ewing, aja monet, Mariame Kaba, Naomi Klein, Rebecca Solnit, Olúfẹ́mi O. Táíwò, Mohammed El-Kurd, José Olivarez, Noam Chomsky, Winona LaDuke, Robyn Maynard, Leanne Betasamosake Simpson, Howard Zinn, Mike Davis, Marc Lamont Hill, Dave Zirin, Astra Taylor, and Amy Goodman, among many other leading writers of our time. We are also the trade publishers of the acclaimed Historical Materialism Book Series.

Haymarket also manages a vibrant community organizing and event space in Chicago, Haymarket House, the popular Haymarket Books Live event series and podcast, and the annual Socialism Conference.